U.S. Army Aviatio

Written by Wayne Mutza

Cover Art by Don Greer

Line Illustrations by Matheu Spraggins

Squadron Signal Publications

(Front Cover) No element of Army Aviation in Vietnam better illustrates close combat than the OH-6A "Loach," teamed with an AH-1G Cobra gunship, forming a lethal "Pink Team." Loach crews often worked below tree level, trading blows with the enemy.

(Back Cover, Top) The Army Security Agency played a major role in Southeast Asia, using a variety of fixed-wing and rotary-wing aircraft for signal intelligence. Operating under the Radio Research title, aircraft often displayed the feline theme based on project systems abbreviations.

(Back Cover, Bottom) Under the auspices of the Army Concept Team in Vietnam (ACTIV), the Utility Tactical Transport Helicopter Company brought the armed UH-1 to Vietnam to evaluate the famed Huey with various weapons and paint schemes. This UH-1B carried 76 rockets in four launchers.

ISBN 978-0-89747-596-9

Military/Combat Photographs

If you have any photos of aircraft, armor, soldiers, or ships of any nation, particularly wartime snapshots, why not share them with us and help make Squadron/Signal's books all the more interesting and complete in the future? Any photograph sent to us will be copied and returned. Electronic images are preferred. The donor will be fully credited for any photos used. Please send them to:

Squadron/Signal Publications
1115 Crowley Drive, Carrollton, TX 75006-1312 U.S.A.
Printed in the U.S.A.
www.SquadronSignalPublications.com

About the Special Series

Squadron/Signal Publications' most open-ended genre of books, our Special category features a myriad of subjects that include unit histories, military campaigns, aircraft, ships, armor, and uniforms. Upcoming subjects include war heroes and non-military areas of interest. If you have an idea for a book or are interested in authoring one, please let us know.

Acknowledgments

This book would not have been possible without help provided by the following: Al Adcock, John A. Agnew, Neil Aird, Don Brabec, Robert Brackenhoff, Robert J. Brandt, Dennis Buley, Wayne Buser, Larry Davis, Dick Detra, Leo Faciane, Karl E. Hayes, David E. Jones, Gene Kennedy, Terry Love, Lennart Lundh, Stephen Miller, Hugh Mills, Gary Rousch, Larry D. Smith, Robert N. Steinbrunn, Larry Vetterman, Floyd S. Werner, and Frank White.

Dedication

This book is dedicated to the Richard I. Bong Chapter of the International Plastic Modelers Society.

(Title Page) A UH-1D Huey of the 1st Flight Platoon, 118th Assault Helicopter Company flies protectively over U.S. Army infantry troops fighting a battle in a South Vietnamese village in 1967. The Huey would far surpass its utility designation, becoming the very symbol of the Vietnam war. (U.S. Army)

Airmobile

The forefathers of U.S. Army aviation endured a great deal of frustration and opposition as they shaped what became one of the world's largest and most efficient air arms. Following World War II, inter-service rivalry choked off funds for the development, and even the testing of equipment, for an Army helicopter force. Despite budget shortcomings and trial and error fraught with growing pains during the Korean War, a dozen Sikorsky H-19s proved the theory of rapid deployment using helicopters. In October 1951, in just under six hours, they moved nearly 1,000 soldiers to relieve others on a 3,000-foot high ridge. Next came experiments with arming helicopters.

During the mid 1950s, Major General James Gavin coined the term "Air Cavalry," which defined the use of helicopters to move troops, and then back them up with armed aircraft. Gavin's ideas came to fruition in Vietnam, where Army aviation grew to enormous dimensions as its participants wrote the book on "Airmobility."

Ever watchful over their domain, the Air Force since its inception in 1947 expressed its desire to have limits placed on the numbers and types of Army aircraft. That concern became obvious when Air Force officials bristled over the large numbers of aircraft and personnel in the Army's 1952 budget. An agreement signed that year prohibiting the Army from duplicating air missions of the Air Force was often side-stepped by Army brass. Inter-service rivalry abounded and it was endless. Adding to the frustration of Army leaders were early Army experiments with air mobility and aircraft that showed little promise.

As for helicopters, specifically, Army staff got serious about them in 1949, a stance that would pay dividends in the years to come. Since the Korean War, it had not become lost on Army leaders that

The U.S. Army trainer version of the Bell H-13 "Sioux" was the TH-13T. At Fort Eustis, Virginia, in 1972, s/n 66-8062 sports the overall International Orange paint and large white ID codes that were standard on Army trainer aircraft. (Stephen Miller)

This OH-23G, s/n 61-3207, was a three-seat, dual-control version of Hiller's family of "Raven" helicopters. The OH-23G joined the Bell Sioux in shouldering the Aeroscout mission in Vietnam prior to the OH-6A's arrival. (Dick Van Allen)

Most common among the trainers used for Warrant Officer Candidate flight instruction was the Hughes TH-55A "Osage," affectionately dubbed the "Mattel Messerschmitt." Nearly 800 TH-55As were built, the majority of which helped Army rotary-wing pilots earn their wings. (Dick Van Allen)

their aviation assets were indispensable. The period after 1952 saw the rapid expansion and change of Army aviation, including the establishment of helicopter units. By the end of the decade, Army aviation became a specialized field, in which the inventory of both fixed and rotary-wing aircraft more than tripled. New ideas were in the air and the terms "Air Assault" and "Airmobility" were heard. Experiments with aerial weapons and establishment of an aerial combat reconnaissance unit in 1958 announced the independence and strength of Army aviation.

As the situation in Vietnam worsened, the U.S. Army Tactical Mobility Requirements Board (called the "Howze Board" after its chairman) was formed in early 1962. The Howze Board was to re-examine the role of Army aviation and aircraft requirements, based on Secretary of Defense Robert McNamara's surprising recommendation for "...a plan for employment of fresh and perhaps unorthodox concepts which will give us a significant increase in mobility." In three months the Howze Board came to a single major conclusion: that the airmobile concept was necessary. The Board recognized the air assault division as the principal innovation, leading to formation of the 11th Air Assault Division, which, on 1 July 1965, became the 1st Cavalry Division (Airmobile).

Regardless of the Air Force's expected disapproval, the war was on and the "Cav" was ordered to Vietnam. The massive division comprised nearly 16,000 men and 434 aircraft, all of which were helicopters except for six OV-1 Mohawks. Within weeks, the 1st Cav was bloodied in what became known as the Battle of the Ia Drang Valley. During the 35-day battle, 54,000 sorties were flown, with 59 helicopters hit by ground fire and 11 crewmen killed. Entire infantry and artillery battalions were moved by air, proving the concept of airmobility.

The only other airmobile division to serve in Vietnam was the 101st Airborne Division. Infantry divisions had an aviation battalion and an air cavalry troop. To command and standardize the growing number of Army aviation units in Vietnam, the 1st Aviation Brigade was formed in May 1966, encompassing all non-divisional aviation units. Besides these major organizations were numerous units that served command and support elements. The exception was the 11th Air Cavalry Regiment, to which an air cavalry troop was assigned. The basic types of unit upon which the airmobile concept was designed were the Assault Helicopter Company (AHC), the Assault Support Helicopter Company (ASHC) and the Air Cavalry Troop. As the number of helicopters swelled, larger numbers of fixed-wing aircraft, such as the OV-1 Mohawk and CV-2 Caribou, were appearing on the Army inventory. Turbine power changed the face of Army aviation. The success of air mobility forced the enemy to increase his effort, and so it went until the drawn-out chain of events culminated in an enormous U.S. Army aviation organization. The quagmire that was Vietnam became known as "The Helicopter War," for fling-wing soldiers dominated the unfriendly skies of South Vietnam.

Besides worldwide commitments, the Army tried to keep pace with the war's expansion, while the units of various types became dependent on one another and formed a vast network throughout South Vietnam. Light fixed-wing aircraft supported command elements, operated as Forward Air Controllers (FACs), and established a country-wide supply net. Still others conducted surveillance in the shadows. Heavier and more sophisticated fixed-wing "Mohawks," "Caribous," and even the Lockheed P2V "Neptunes," were added to the mix, only to become burrs in the saddles of Air Force leaders. Transport helicopters became necessary

While large numbers of Hueys went to war in Vietnam, Army leaders were mindful of worldwide commitments. This early UH-1B shares ramp space with a CH-34 at Mannheim, Germany in 1969, the war's peak year. Painted overall gloss black, the Huey served as a VIP transport, complete with plush interior, cabin boarding step, and FM radio antennas. (Robert Brackenhoff)

In cavalry tradition, a mounted officer in cavalry dress was part of the ceremony converting the 11th Air Assault Division to the 1st Cavalry Division (Airmobile) at Fort Benning, Georgia in July 1965. The Stetson hat became an enduring symbol of Cavalry officers in Vietnam. (Ed Lemp)

to move Army Republic of Vietnam (ARVN) troops. The glaring need for medical evacuation brought to Vietnam the first Hueys, which soon would take center stage as the primary transport vehicle and gunship. The powerful CH-47 "Chinook" followed, replacing the CH-37 for downed aircraft recovery. The CH-54 "Tarhe," better known as the "Skycrane," would prove itself the ultimate heavy lifter. The tiny Hughes OH-6A "Loach", along with its equally impressive and fearsome partner, Bell's AH-1G "Cobra," the first pure gunship, wrote other chapters in Army aviation history. The designs of many of these aircraft were tailored to the war, which became the ultimate proving ground. The Chinook still serves as a frontline aircraft in today's Army, while the Cobra thrives in the Marine Corps.

Hughes officials have avowed that were it not for the research and development that produced the Loach, the present day "Apache" gunship would not have been born.

Army aviation in Vietnam generally operated in conjunction with ground units, its pilot cadre initially comprising branch officers who were familiar with utilizing aviation assets. With its assets spread thin in Europe, Korea, and Vietnam, the Army in 1966 suffered from a serious pilot shortage. It didn't help that Army aviators in Vietnam were given the additional duties of training U.S. Naval aircrews in the armed Huey to support "Market Time" operations in Vietnam's waterways. Also that year Army pilots were directed to begin training South Vietnamese Air Force (VNAF) pilots in the Huey. Relief came by moving more Warrant Officers through the training pipeline. Eventually the U.S. Army Primary Helicopter School at Fort Wolters, Texas, was turning out a record 600 Warrant Officer Candidate (WOC) pilots per month. The number of helicopters at the school peaked in 1969 at more than 1,300, which comprised Hughes TH-55As, Bell OH-13s, and Hiller OH-23s.

In Vietnam pilots were flying up to 120 hours per month, far exceeding the safe limit. Fatigue became a major factor in accident rates. It was not unusual for Hueys to log more than double the

Protected against weather and salt water corrosion, UH-1 Hueys and CH-47 Chinooks of the 1st Cavalry Division are aboard the USS Boxer waiting to deploy to Vietnam in September 1965. (Ed Lemp)

The transportation companies (TCs) that brought CH-21s to Vietnam eventually camouflaged their aircraft. The first unit to arrive, the 8th TC, removed the CH-21s' vertical stabilizers to reduce weight, although airspeed then had to be cut to 70 knots. This 8th TC Shawnee sports new camouflage in March 1963. A white and orange strip, along with the original national insignia on the upper fuselage, helped higher-flying aircraft keep the CH-21 in sight. (Richard Bumstead via Robert J. Brandt)

accepted 70 hours of flight per month. Pilots often taught crew chiefs how to fly aircraft so they could fly as co-pilot on non-combat flights, or if the pilot was wounded or killed. Not only crew chiefs, but door gunners, mechanics, avionics, and armament specialists were in critical demand. Crew chiefs and gunners often flew all day only to work on the aircraft through the night. Pilots respected the unique bond that crew chiefs formed with their aircraft.

Although the Vietnam experience emphasized the continuing controversy of tactical air support versus helicopter gunship, ground commanders usually found choppers more responsive, yet they regarded both as having their own respective merits. Enemy opposition was so fierce that whichever type was available would be called in. Beginning in 1965, 11 Huey and Cobra-equipped units were regularly assigned direct support of special operations, often during cross-border missions.

Other than a flight detachment of the Military Assistance Advisory Group based at Saigon since the mid 1950s, the first U.S. Army aviation units sent to Vietnam were the 8th and 57th Transportation Companies (TC). Equipped with 20 CH-21 Shawnee and two OH-13E Sioux helicopters each, the two light helicopter units arrived at Saigon Port on 11 December 1961. Operating from Tan Son Nhut Airport, members of the 8th and 57th began training the ARVN in airmobile operations, while themselves learning by trial and error. Especially frustrating were

Often overlooked is the participation of Army fixed-wing aircraft in the "Helicopter War." Wearing high-visibility schemes, aircraft such as this U-8D at Da Nang in 1965, operated in Southeast Asia as early as the 1950s. (David Menard)

Locally-applied camouflage is apparent on this CH-21C in 1963. Efforts to protect the aircraft during troop insertions included .30 cal. machine guns, such as this gun on a swing-out mount, later used on Hueys. The name "Tiki 2" appears next to a caricature of an island native. (Al Adcock)

CH-21Cs of the 121st Aviation Company are escorted by a USAF T-28 and a UH-1B in 1963. Visible on the CH-21 in the foreground (s/n 51-15902) is the tiger emblem of the 121st, formerly the 93rd Transportation Company. Often overlooked are the CH-21's abilities, which led to the rapid expansion of Army aviation in Vietnam. Although replaced by the turbine-powered UH-1B Huey, the CH-21 could carry more weight, fly faster when fully loaded, and, most importantly, could carry a complete infantry squad. (U.S. Army)

parts shortages and increased maintenance as a result of Vietnam's high humidity. The first joint exercise was held on 22 December, with the first air assault taking place on 2 January 1962, when the two companies carried more than 1,000 ARVN soldiers into a small jungle landing zone (LZ). Although there was little contact with the enemy, the potential of airmobility had been demonstrated.

Late in January the CH-21-equipped 93rd TC arrived, taking up station at Da Nang Air Base to cover northern I Corps. In April the 57th Medical Detachment brought the first Hueys to Vietnam. That same month the first U.S. Marine Corps helicopters arrived. Throughout 1962 the flow of units increased; 10 more Hueys arrived in May, the 18th Aviation Company brought its fixed-wing Otters to establish a supply network, and the Shawnee-equipped 33rd and 81st TCs came in September, the same month that the controversial Mohawks appeared. Caribous began flying supply hops and the following spring, Bird Dog FACs were dotting the sky, and helicopters dedicated to aircraft recovery became a reality. The year 1962 also saw the arrival of the Utility Tactical Transport Helicopter Company (UTTCHO), which served as armed escorts. As a test unit with 15 UH-1As, the UTTHCO was writing the book on gunships while laying down ordnance to protect CH-21 transports. By year's end, 13 Army aviation units were in country, flying 200 aircraft of eight different types.

At the beginning of 1965 there were 250 Hueys in Vietnam. That year would be a turning point in the war, with the arrival of U.S. ground troops to counter overt enemy action against Americans. The arrival of the 173rd Airborne Brigade in May signaled the transition from America's support role to one of defense. The following month, that switched to an offensive mode when the 173rd took part in the largest lift operation of the war. A total of 144 helicopters flew into War Zone D, where allied forces had not set foot for a year. Shortly thereafter, elements of the 101st Airborne Division and the 1st Infantry Division took up residence in Vietnam.

Over the course of the war, airmobile operations were improved and aircraft upgraded to keep pace with the ever-changing tactical environment. Throughout Vietnam's four Corps Tactical Zones, airmobile forces quickly took the battle to the enemy, or they cut off his escape following hit-and-run attacks. In April 1970 the 1st Cavalry Division launched its Cambodian campaign, marking the first time a large-scale operation took place outside Vietnam's borders. Cavalry units struck deep into the enemy's sanctuaries, catching him off balance and demonstrating the airmobile concept better than on any previous operation. The next year saw another operation in the same region and an invasion of Laos. Code-named Lam Son 719, the two-month combined operation launched on 8 February 1971, was the final large-scale airmobile operation of the war. Lam Son targeted North Vietnamese base areas in Laos and the Ho Chi Minh Trail supply route. The enemy responded aggressively, committing a variety of weapons, including tanks, to the battle. Armor again appeared when the enemy initiated the 1972 "Easter Invasion." Since the lessons of Lam Son had led to anti-armor weapons tests, three UH-1Bs mounting TOW anti-armor missiles, which had been sent to Vietnam prior to the attack, claimed 26 armor kills, 10 alone in one day.

The Army aviation organization in Vietnam had a unique and elaborate system of aircraft markings and camouflage. Since the 11th Air Assault Division was formed in 1963 to generate new ideas, it was decided that special markings would make aircraft quickly identifiable to ground troops, and strengthen the relationship between them and air crew. Thus began a pattern of unit designators, usually in the form of geometric shapes. The 1st Aviation Brigade followed suit after it was organized, as did the 101st Airborne Division. The use of geometric shapes spread to other aviation units until nearly every Army aircraft in Vietnam wore geometric shapes, numbers, and stripes mainly on their doors, tails, noses, and cabin roofs. Group, battalion, squadron, company, and troop markings became common. Personal markings also flourished on Army aircraft. Sharkmouths were in abundance, yet distinctive enough to identify units. At the war's onset, Army aircraft were painted Gloss Olive Drab with high visibility markings.

These were sprayed over, and many units, especially those flying CH-21s and UH-1Bs, experimented with camouflage, usually adding black and brown to the overall Olive Drab. In 1965 the Army ordered aircraft painted in a low-visibility scheme of Flat Olive

Throughout the war, Army fixed-wing aircraft flew uncamouflaged like this U-8F in VIP scheme. Serial number 62-3867 belonged to U.S. Army Republic of Vietnam Headquarters and is seen here at Tan Son Nhut Air Base in 1967. (Terry Love)

A Beech U-21A (s/n 61-8029) at Tan Son Nhut AB in 1967. Such aircraft flew a wide range of missions vital to the Army's logistics network throughout Southeast Asia. (Terry Love)

Drab with black markings. Camouflaged aircraft were difficult to see from above, so units began painting the upper surfaces of aircraft in various colors. In mid-1967, a directive called for a white 36-inch band on top of main rotors. A 1969 directive changed that to an all-white blade, with the other painted black. In addition, the upper surfaces of helicopter elevators were to be painted Red-Orange. During the late 1960s, battalion and company numbers were added to the tops of elevators, and buzz numbers were applied to their under surfaces.

The number of U.S. Army helicopters in Vietnam peaked at 3,926 in March 1970, giving the U.S. Army the world's third-largest air force. Throughout the 11 years of war, about 13,000 Army aircraft flew Vietnam's skies. From 1961 to 1973, the epic of Army aviation in Vietnam was written, often in blood, by legions of aircraft crews and support personnel. Some Army aviators, Medal of Honor recipients, commanders, and pioneers of Army aviation, have been widely recognized, while others passed silently into history following their Vietnam experience.

During the early 1960s, the Army purchased more than 20 U-10 Helio Couriers, which were used mainly to support Army Special Forces operations in Southeast Asia. Some flew from Udorn Royal Thai Air Force Base (RTAFB) to support SF missions in Laos. In keeping with such covert duty, this U-10B wore a low-profile scheme. In the hands of an experienced short takeoff and landing (STOL) pilot, the Helio Courier could almost hover in a strong wind, making it ideal for operations from rugged strips in mountainous regions. (Robert Brackenhoff)

Bird Dogs

The use of light aircraft for Forward Air Control (FAC) is commonly associated with the U.S. Air Force, although such missions in Vietnam were first flown by U.S. Army and VNAF L-19 Bird Dog aircraft. The concept of using light aircraft to direct artillery and air strikes is nothing new, having been developed during World War Two.

Both the U.S. Army and Air Force flew FAC missions during the Korean war; the Army with small observation-type "L" planes, and the Air Force flying T-6 "Texans."

The first Bird Dogs in Vietnam had arrived with the French Army during the early 1950s. Since Vietnam's forbidding terrain dictated the need for observation aircraft, the CH-21 units that began arriving in 1961 each had two Bell H-13 "Sioux" helicopters assigned. Although the Sioux later performed well in the scout role, it could not keep up with the CH-21s, and it did not have the range for reconnaissance or mission planning.

The H-13s were returned to the U.S. and replaced by Cessna TL-19Ds (later TO-1Ds), setting the stage for their widespread use throughout the war.

The L-19 itself was a rugged and versatile aircraft, having excellent short field capability. It featured superb visibility, reasonable endurance, and it was easy to maintain.

It was the first aircraft procured specifically for the Army, with deliveries beginning in 1950, in time for the Korean war. The L-19s went to work on the Korean front lines in February 1951, finding targets, spotting for artillery, re-supplying units, and transporting personnel. Until Cessna's T-41 "Mescalero" appeared in 1966, the Bird Dog had been the Army's primary fixed-wing trainer.

With combat missions in Vietnam on the rise, early transport helicopter pilots found it difficult to navigate at low level over rough terrain, proving the need for high-flying controller aircraft. Various types of aircraft were used to scout for the enemy and plan safe routes until more Bird Dogs arrived.

Eventually, one dozen Army Bird Dog units would serve in Vietnam. First among them was the 73rd Aviation Company (Airplane Surveillance Light), which arrived by ship at Saigon during May 1963. With 22 O-1Ds, the 73rd was temporarily based at Vung Tau under the 45th Transportation Battalion. Ten O-1Ds transferred from CH-21 units brought the 73rd up to its full complement of 32 Bird Dogs. The aircraft were dispersed to 15 locations to fulfill the reconnaissance needs of U.S. advisors. The unit then moved to Nha Trang, and on 1 October 1964 it was divided into four detachments for assignment to the aviation battalion in each Corps area.

The "Warriors" of the 73rd flew a variety of missions, including artillery adjustment, target acquisition, re-supply, and radio relay for ground units. On some occasions the 73rd carried out medevac operations. Underwing stores included Mk-6 flares, fragmentation bomb clusters, KS-54 camera pods, and supply bundles for Special Forces teams. Soon members of the 73rd had established their own school to train Vietnamese pilots and observers, while writing the book on surveillance in Vietnam.

During their first 14 months in Vietnam, 73rd flight crews amassed more than 41,000 flight hours.

Initially, company policy held that Bird Dogs not fly below 1,500

A TO-1D (s/n 57-2832) of the 73rd Aviation Company at Tay Ninh in September 1963. In contrast to the Bird Dog's high visibility markings, CH-21s of the 57th TC overhead wear camouflage. (William McGee)

During the early 1960s, this pair of O-1Ds was attached to the 117th Aviation Company, which painted its UH-1B helicopters a similar camouflage pattern of brown and black over Olive Drab. (Author's Collection)

The CH-21 units that were early arrivals in Vietnam each had between two and four Bird Dogs assigned. This pair of TO-1Ds belonged to the 33rd TC (Light Helicopter) at Bien Hoa AB in 1962 and 1963. Both later went to the 73rd Aviation Company, with 57-2933 becoming a combat loss. (Kenneth D. Stanton via Robert J. Brandt)

Bird Dogs of the 120th Aviation Company wear camouflage like this TO-1D, s/n 57-2921, in 1963. The leading upper wing edges are white, for overhead visibility. The white mortarboard on the tail reflects the 120th's nickname: "The Deans." (Elof S. Lundh)

This O-1D (s/n 57-2832) of the 73rd ASL in 1963 wears nine purple hearts, underscoring the danger of low-level work. (Elof S. Lundh)

feet when alone, and that field glasses be used. Aircrew quickly learned that to do their job, they had to fly "on the deck," 100 feet and lower. Bird Dog pilots and observers found targets that aircrew in faster aircraft could not. FAC pilots became intimately familiar with their assigned sectors, and became skilled in observation techniques, learning to develop and trust their senses. They became adept at *reading sign,* noticing details such as footprints, changes in scenery, and habits of villagers and farmers.

If a FAC was not already overhead supporting troops on the ground, the nearest one joined the Tac-Air forces summoned by troops who came under attack. FAC pilots had to perform numerous functions, usually under adverse conditions. Their judgment and responsibility in directing the destructive power at their beckon was awesome. Even the tenacious enemy came to respect the little airplane, knowing that to shoot at it and reveal his position meant his demise. Later the enemy decided to try to shoot down the FAC to ruin the effectiveness of the strike that was sure to follow.

With the massive buildup of U.S. forces in Vietnam came the need for large numbers of Bird Dogs. Accordingly, more than 500 L-19As and TL-19Ds went to Cessna for modifications to prepare them for combat. The TL-19Ds had their cockpit heaters and rear training instrument panels removed. Two bomb racks were installed under each wing to accommodate eight rockets. Changes in avionics equipment included the addition of a UHF radio for communication with strike aircraft. Twenty-two of the aircraft, which were called O-1Ds, went to the U.S. Air Force to meet an urgent need for FAC aircraft. Model L-19As (O-1As) that underwent modifications for combat were labeled O-1Es. Serving both the Army and Air Force in Vietnam, the O-1E was the result of having trainer features removed, and the addition of radio gear, self-sealing fuel tanks, armored pilots' seats, and underwing racks. These changes, along with structural strengthening, brought the aircraft's weight up to 2,400 pounds.

In late 1964, the OV-1 Mohawk-equipped 23rd Special Warfare Aviation Detachment assumed the 73rd designation, and the unit's O-1s eventually were absorbed by the 74th Aviation Company. Using the call sign "Aloft," the 74th set up shop at Phu Loi, staying in Vietnam until 1972. The 219th, 220th, and 221st Aviation Companies

A pair of O-1As (s/n 51-4611 and 51-12002) of the 219th RAC stand alert at Ban Me Thuot in September 1971. Their 17th Combat Aviation Group tail markings were enhanced by a blue field with nine white stars. (James R. Wagner)

arrived during July 1965, followed by the 131st, 183rd, and 184th in 1966, and the 21st, 199th, 185th, and 203rd during 1967. In 1966 these units were re-designated Reconnaissance Airplane Companies (RAC).

Some units felt that the O-1 fell short of FAC mission requirements, calling the airplane noisy, underpowered, especially in mountainous regions, and noting that it wasn't as easily maintained as expected, and it lacked forward visibility. To give them an edge in combat, Bird Dog crews tried various forms of offensive armament, including fragmentation bomb clusters, 7-shot rocket launchers, and machine guns fired from the cabin. Missions considered high risk often were flown by two O-1s. The concept of arming Bird Dogs with target-marking rockets was born in 1965, when pilots grew concerned about the danger of over-flying targets to drop smoke grenades. Bolstering the idea was a recommendation in 1965 by pilots of the 2nd Battalion, 20th Artillery of the 1st Cavalry Division that O-1s equipped with rockets mark LZs prior to combat assaults.

Rockets used to mark targets were of the white phosphorous variety, called "Willy Petes." Ground troops depended on the Bird Dog to the extent that one of the 219th's four platoons was assigned to Command and Control Central of the classified Studies and Observation Group (SOG), becoming part of the *Sneaky Pete Air Force.*

As the war gained momentum and the Air Force became largely responsible for air strikes, Air Force planners sought a strike control and observation aircraft. While the optimum aircraft to fill this role was being developed, the Bird Dog was selected as an interim FAC platform. As O-1s were being transferred to the Air Force, the Army's 1st Aviation Brigade in late 1966 began a program to maximize use of the O-1s in Vietnam.

Army pilots were trained in target marking for air strikes, and

The popular shark mouth was not limited to Army helicopters. This O-1E (s/n 56-2688) of the 183rd Aviation Company sported the marking in 1966. The Bird Dog also wears the company seahorse emblem on its engine cowl, and the emblem of the parent unit, the 223rd Aviation Battalion, on the tail. (Terry Love)

Despite sand bag protection, this 199th Aviation Company O-1A (s/n 51-12904) named "Cosmo's Camel" was destroyed together with a USAF O-1 during a ground attack at Rach Gia on 28 November 1967. (Charles W. Baker via Jim Burridge)

This O-1G (s/n 51-12241), assigned to the 199th RAC, has the 214th Combat Aviation Battalion emblem on its tail. Four 2.75-inch rocket launchers for target marking were standard under Army Bird Dog wings. (Larry Davis Collection)

Air Force pilots learned artillery and naval gunfire adjustment techniques.

The ideal FAC aircraft in Vietnam was said to have parachute ejection, speed and a high rate of climb, armor, and plenty of ordnance. To the Bird Dog's credit, such an airplane not only lacked the ability to work low and slow, it couldn't match the O-1's ability to operate from short, rough fields. Numerous accounts tell of the determination and skill of Bird Dog pilots, who stubbornly stayed with their charges who were under attack, or downed flyers awaiting rescue.

The Army's plan to replace the Bird Dog during 1970 lost momentum with the transfer of the type to the Air Force. Instead, the Army's reconnaissance needs were fulfilled by the OV-1 Mohawk and the combat-proven Hughes OH-6A helicopter.

As testimony to their importance, O-1s of the U.S. Army, Air Force and Marine Corps accounted for the second largest loss of fixed-wing aircraft during the war, surpassed only by F-4 Phantoms. Of nearly 470 Bird Dogs destroyed, 284 were Army aircraft, 82 of which were downed by small arms fire, 27 lost to ground attack, and 175 deemed operational losses. Although relatively easy to handle in the air, Bird Dogs were less forgiving on the ground, evidenced by numerous ground loops.

An imposing statue and a Bird Dog propeller leave no doubt that one is entering the zone of the 219th Aviation Company "Headhunters." Such dramatic displays said much about the character and morale of combat units. (Rodger D. Fetters)

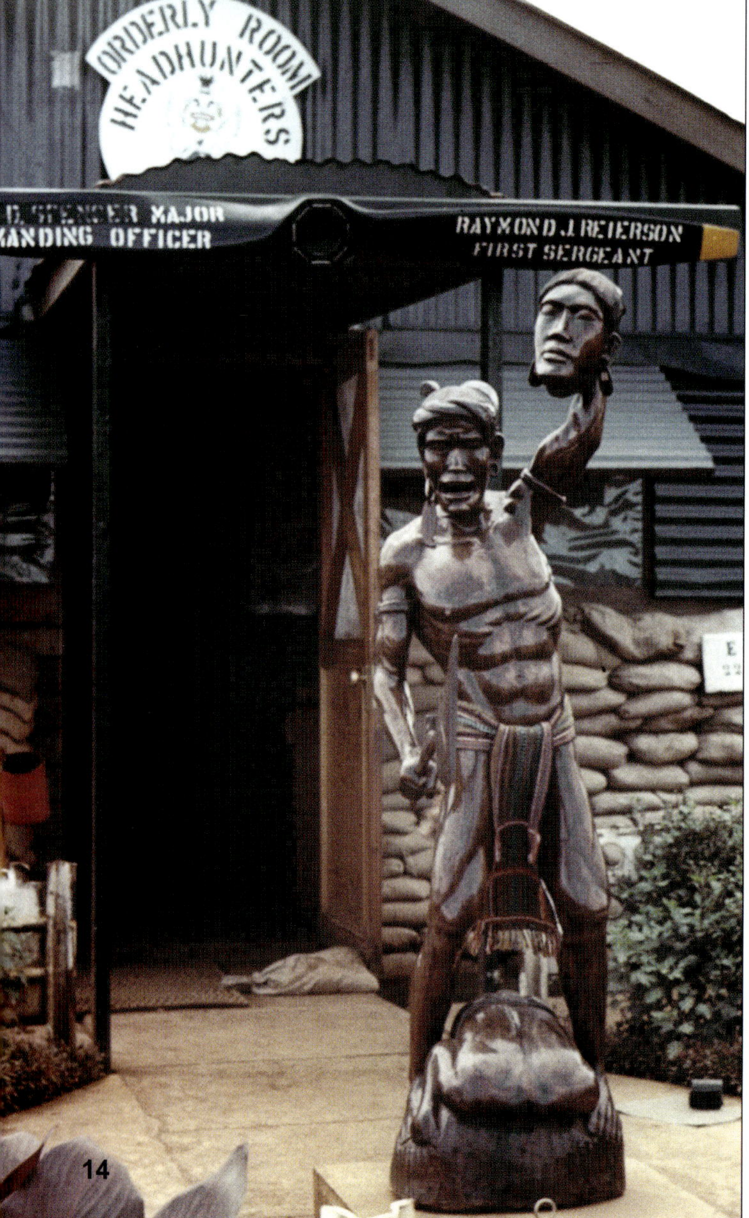

U.S. Army Bird Dog Aviation Companies in Vietnam

Unit	In Vietnam	Location	Call Sign
21st	June '67-Nov. '71	Chu lai	Black Ace, Cat, Bird Dog
73rd	May '63-late '64	Nha Trang	Warrior, Observe
74th	Mar. '65-Mar. '72	Phu Loi	Aloft
131st	June '66-July '71	Hue-Phu Bai	Nighthawk
183rd	June '66-Nov. '71	Dong Ba Thinh	Seahorse
184th	Aug. '66-July '71	Phu Loi	Non-stop
185th	June '67-Oct. '70	Ban Me Thuot	Pterodactyl
199th	July '67-Oct. '70	Vinh Long	Hawkeye, Swamp Fox
203rd	Oct. '67-Apr. '71	Phu Hiep, Tuy Hoa	Hawkeye
219th	June '65-Dec. '71	Pleiku	Headhunter
220th	July '65-Dec. '71	Hue-Phu Bai	Catkiller
221st	July '65-Nov. '71	Soc Trang	Shotgun

(Above) Bird Dogs of the 199th Aviation Company wore their "Swamp Fox" emblem on the forward fuselage. (Larry Davis Collection)

(Right) Seen at Quin Nhon, this TO-1D (s/n 57-2841) was downed during a low-level mission when its pilot was killed by a single bullet fired at the aircraft. The observer was injured in the incident. By the mid 1960s, high-visibility markings, which the enemy used as aiming points, were replaced by fewer markings, which were also more subdued. (Don Wisniewski via David Hansen)

(Below) This TO-1D of the 73rd Aviation Company departs the strip at Ban Me Thuot during the early 1960s with parachute-rigged supply containers under its wings. Bird Dogs often flew in support of small commando teams, many of which operated from Ban Me Thuot. (Al Adcock)

One of the Army's early ambitions in Vietnam was to arm its Mohawks, thereby expanding their surveillance role to include attack. When the Air Force challenged such infringement on its air superiority, the weapons were eventually removed. Some OV-1s, however, retained armament - as Army officials claimed - for self defense. This OV-1 of the 73rd Aviation Company wears on its tail fin in 1968 the white "X" symbol of the 222nd Combat Aviation Battalion. (Author's Collection)

Mohawks, Cuties, and YO-YOs

Knowing the importance of aerial observation, Army planners in 1954 announced their requirement for a high performance observation aircraft. Since the Marines had begun searching for a replacement for their Cessna Bird Dog, they, represented by the Navy, joined Army officials in planning the new aircraft. The Marines specified that the aircraft have a light attack capability, however, they dropped out of the program, leaving the Army with Grumman's two-seat, twin turboprop OV-1 "Mohawk." The OV-1 could operate in all weather, at night, and from unimproved fields. Although the Mohawk, along with the Caribou, was exempt from the 5,000-pound weight restriction placed on Army aircraft to prevent duplicating missions of the Air Force, its armament fittings carried over from the Marine requirement would prove vexing to the Air Force.

Seen at Vung Tau in 1966, this Mohawk of the 73rd SAC is armed with 19-shot, 2.75-inch rocket launchers, and .50 cal. machine gun pods. (Terry Love)

Wearing the name "Newt's Dream" under the cockpit, this OV-1C (s/n 61-2712) rests on the transient ramp at Da Nang AB in 1966. Tail markings indicate that the Mohawk, call sign "Spud 23," belonged to the 131st SAC based at Phu Bai. External 150-gallon fuel tanks extended the OV-1's endurance to 4 hours, 30 minutes. (Tom Hansen)

The Mohawk was a star performer and it became an early participant in the Vietnam war. Mohawks equipped with the full complement of six under-wing armament mounts were designated JOV-1As. Six of these were assigned to the 23rd Special Warfare Aviation Detachment (SWAD), which arrived in Vietnam in September 1962. Before the end of November, the 23rd would be divided into three teams of two aircraft each to operate where best able to provide support throughout II Corps. On missions, these Mohawks were restricted to mounting .50 cal. machine guns, and they were allowed to fire only when fired upon. In addition, the observer was to be Vietnamese.

Flying mainly in support of the South Vietnamese Army, the visual and photographic surveillance provided by the OV-1s went a long way in prohibiting enemy activity. A distinct advantage of the Mohawk was its ability to approach the enemy relatively unheard, thanks to its speed and quiet engines. The Mohawk's quick reaction time, surveillance capabilities, and armament won favor with ground commanders, who used them to full advantage. The accuracy and amount of artillery fire increased greatly after the Mohawk's arrival in Vietnam. As OV-1s proved their value in armed close air support, pilots and ground commanders shared the belief that OV-1 armament be increased. Accordingly, during early 1963, 2.75-inch rocket launchers were added to the Mohawk's muscle, a move that made Air Force leaders bristle in the wake of turbulence over Army and Air Force tactical responsibility.

After additional Mohawks arrived with the 4th Aerial Surveillance and Target Acquisition (ASTA) Detachment during late 1964, its OV-1Bs and OV-1Cs were combined with those of the 23rd SWAD to form the 73rd Aviation Company (Aerial Surveillance). By mid-1965, the 73rd boasted nearly 30 Mohawks, comprising OV-1A, JOV-1A, OV-1B, and OV-1C models. The OV-1B introduced Side-Looking Airborne Radar (SLAR), along with other improvements including strengthened wings, weight reductions, and updated engines and electronics. The OV-1C featured improved camera systems and infrared surveillance capabilities.

During late 1965, three additional Mohawk units arrived in Vietnam: the ASTA Platoon of the 1st Cavalry Division's 11th Aviation Company went to An Khe; the 20th ASTA Detachment "Night Hawks" set up shop at Nha Trang; and the ASTA Platoon, B Company, 1st Aviation Battalion, 1st Infantry Division "Hawk Eyes" was established at Phu Loi. Despite the dismay of the Air Force over air support responsibilities, in December 1965 the Air Force launched *Operation Tiger Hand*, in which Mohawks made night flights over the Ho Chi Minh Trail locating targets that were illuminated by accompanying Air Force C-130 flareships. The 20th ASTA lived up to its nickname "Night Hawks" by flying missions throughout the night, proving to the enemy that they no longer could rely on the cover of darkness.

The Mohawk-equipped 131st Aviation Company, which was attached to the 1st Cavalry Division, took over 20th ASTA assets in June 1966. The 225th "Phantom Hawks" arrived at Phu Hiep in may 1967. The 244th "Delta Hawks" arrived at Can Tho in July 1967, and Mohawk assets in Vietnam reached their peak in October 1967 with the arrival at Da Nang of the 245th Aviation Company "Red

Eye." In 1969 Mohawk units were designated *Surveillance Airplane Companies (SAC)*.

Despite relentless Air Force opposition to armed Mohawks, some remained armed with rockets for self defense. Mohawks of the 131st SAC, which operated from Phu Bai, were seen with rocket launchers as late as 1971. The 131st used its OV-1Bs for missions over the DMZ, Cambodia, and Laos, while supporting the 101st Airborne Division and Marine units in Vietnam with its OV-1As and OV-1Cs.

The success of the Mohawk in providing armed support and surveillance in Vietnam came at a heavy price; 63 OV-1s were lost, 36 to operational causes. Of the 27 combat losses, 26 were shot down, one by a MiG in 1969, becoming the only fixed-wing Army aircraft lost to enemy aircraft. Another was downed in 1966 by a surface-to-air missile, and one was destroyed during a ground attack in 1968.

Unique among the aircraft used in Southeast Asia for surveillance were Lockheed's quiet aircraft designed to see in the night, but not be seen or heard. To address the war zone surveillance issue, and meet the Army requirements for a quiet surveillance platform, Lockheed engineers in 1965 came up with two QT (Quiet Thruster)-2 aircraft. The pair was based on the Schweizer Model SGS 2-32 two-place glider, which had a 57-foot wing span. The Navy inventory listed the glider as the X-26A/B sailplane. Although affectionately dubbed "Cutie," the QT was an ungainly looking craft that could never win a beauty contest. Its four-bladed, fixed-pitch propellers were handcrafted by noted prop specialist Olie Fahlin. These were later replaced by three-bladed, variable pitch props. Power was supplied by a Continental 0-200 100-hp engine that allowed a top speed of 115 mph, and a cruise speed of 75 mph.

Developed under a Lockheed and Army partnership, the QT first flew in July 1967. Later that year it was modified to QT-2PC configuration with a dark gray paint scheme, upgraded avionics, an explosion-proof fuel tank, and observer viewing ports. While the aircraft were being militarized, aircrew was selected from Army, Air Force, and Navy volunteers, who trained with standard Navy X-26As. Labeled *Prize Crew*, the aircraft and personnel were sent in January 1968 to Vietnam for a three-month evaluation period.

Having arrived in time for the Tet Offensive, the QT-2PCs took off nightly from Bien Hoa Air Base, usually detecting fleets of enemy supply sampans in the Mekong Delta.

Success with the QT design led to the construction of 11 YO-3A *Quiet Stars*, the first of which flew in February 1969. From 1970 to 1972 nine *YO-YOs* would conduct nighttime surveillance missions in Southeast Asia. Typically attached to Bird Dog or Mohawk companies, the nine were divided into three teams each with three aircraft, operating mainly from Binh Thuy, Long Thanh North, and Phu Bai to provide maximum coverage. The trio operating from Phu Bai near the DMZ periodically ventured into North Vietnam.

So quiet was the YO-3A that observers reported they never saw enemy troops look skyward as they flew overhead. Pilots sometimes flew directly over enemy positions, dropping white phosphorous grenades to mark targets for inbound strike aircraft. It was also common for YO-3A pilots to fly over mission areas in Bird Dog aircraft during daylight to familiarize themselves with the area. Maximum mission time was six hours, which was all an observer could handle before fatigue set in. Although crashes caused by mechanical problems claimed two Vietnam-based YO-3As, throughout their time in the combat zone, no YO-3As are known to have been fired upon. Serial number 69-18008 was destroyed in a crash, and both crewmen were killed when number 69-18004 crashed near Bien Hoa on 6 June 1971.

"Pandora's Box" was assigned to the 1st Infantry Division Aviation Battalion, B Company, ASTA Platoon at Phu Loi in 1967. Bulged side canopies afforded excellent visibility for the crew of two, who sat side-by-side in ejection seats. (Author's Collection)

Equipped with a night vision system, the YO-3A empty weighed more than 3,000 pounds, requiring a 210-hp engine. Top speed was 138 mph, while slow speed for quieter flight was 70 mph. The pilot sat in the rear and an enlisted observer in the front. The ventral turret housed a wide-angle lens for night vision. This example is seen at Binh Thuy AB in June 1971. (Larry Vetterman)

The later version of the YO-3A with three-bladed prop at Binh Thuy in 1971. Engine noise-silencing apparatus ran the length of the aircraft's fuselage. Although a low-wing aircraft, the YO-3A's large canopy offered the crew excellent visibility. (Larry Vetterman)

The Huey

Not only was the Bell Huey helicopter touted as the key element of the airmobile concept, it became the very symbol of the Vietnam war. The U.S. Army was largely responsible for the Huey's development, which began in 1955. Officially called the "Iroquois," in keeping with the Army tradition of naming aircraft after Native American tribes, the Huey was selected to fill an Army requirement for a new utility helicopter. The Huey owes its success to Bell's pioneering efforts with the turbine engine, which simplified the design and operating characteristics of helicopters.

The first of a long line of Huey models, the HU-1A, first flew in June 1959. For most of its military life, the Huey would be powered by the Lycoming T53 series turbine engine. Following closely on the heels of the A model was the UH-1B, which had more power, a larger cabin to accommodate eight troops, and a larger and improved main rotor system.

Besides a handful of HU-1As deployed to Vietnam for medical evacuation work, a larger number were deployed with the Utility Tactical Transport Helicopter Company in early October 1962. Just six weeks later, 11 UH-1Bs arrived in Vietnam to augment the unit's A models. Both the A and B model Hueys were quickly absorbed into the Army's incessant quest for armed helicopters to provide close support for ground troops.

Initially, Army leaders focused on arming helicopters for use against armor. Early piston-powered helicopters were evaluated with rudimentary armament, and were rated as moderate performers. The Huey changed all that. Its introduction spurred official development of helicopter armament, beginning in March 1957 with a four-machine gun kit for the Huey prototype.

Still of the anti-armor mindset, Army officials in 1958 began tests with the French-developed SS-10 wire-guided missile, and in 1961 SS-11 missiles were ordered for UH-1Bs.

Armament had found a place on Army helicopters. Lift helicopters in Vietnam, which had been escorted by USAF fixed-wing aircraft, now relied on UTTHCO UH-1As armed with .30 cal. machine guns and 2.75-inch rocket launchers. During its evaluation period, the UTTHCO flew 1,779 combat hours, losing one gunship to enemy fire.

As the number of U.S. Army aviation units in Vietnam increased, the first all-Huey assault unit, the 114th Aviation Company (Airmobile Light), arrived during May 1963. The 114th would set the standard for assault helicopter companies by dividing its 25 UH-1s among two lift platoons and an armed gun platoon.

The UH-1D resulted from the Army's decision to upgrade the Huey as a tactical transport. Powered by more powerful versions of Lycoming's T53, this stretched version could carry 14 troops. Deliveries of the "Delta" began in August 1963, with the majority going to the 1st Cavalry's forerunner, the 11th Air Assault Division. Of the 428 helicopters authorized the 1st Cavalry Division, half were UH-1Ds and UH-1Bs. By 1966, a total of 2,008 UH-1Ds had been delivered to the Army. Armed with M-60D crew-operated machine guns, these troop-transport Hueys were nicknamed "Slicks." Delta models were progressively replaced by more powerful UH-1Hs, beginning in September 1967. Over five years, more than 5,000 "Hotel" model Hueys would enter Army service. Of those, 3,375 would serve in Vietnam, 1,313 of which were lost, the highest of any aircraft type. Estimates of the number of all models of Army Hueys that served in Vietnam ranged from over 5,000 to 7,000. More than 10,000 were built during the war years.

Thanks to its superb versatility and the resourcefulness of its crews, the Huey far exceeded its utility classification in Vietnam. Besides its main duties as troop transport and gunship, Hueys performed medical evacuation, flare drops, smoke screening, chemical spraying, command and control, electronic warfare, aircraft recovery, night fighting, bombing, psychological warfare, and surveillance. Countless weapon and miscellaneous systems, both factory-built and fabricated by the units using them, would be

This UH-1B of the 117th Aviation Company (Airmobile Light) was typical of camouflage applied to Army aircraft after they arrived in Vietnam during the early 1960s. Serial number 62-4567 is seen here at Ban Me Thuot, South Vietnam wearing black and tan stripes sprayed onto its original Olive Drab color. (Al Adcock)

"Warrior 21," a UH-1D of A Company, 101st Aviation Battalion at Soc Trang in 1965 displays the Huey high visibility scheme prior to the introduction of the Army's low visibility scheme. The crew chief's M-60 machine gun mount is one of the first types fabricated for the Huey. (George Nonestied)

seen mounted on all Huey models throughout the war.

To capitalize on the use of the Huey as a gunship, and pending the arrival of a pure helicopter gunship, Bell's AH-1G Cobra, the UH-1C was developed as an interim measure. A total of 766 UH-1Cs were produced, all but 10 of which went to the U.S. Army. Although modernization plans called for all C models to be replaced by Cobras, many units flew them to the end of combat operations. Basically an improved B model, the "Charlie" model offered greater all-around performance, thanks to a more powerful engine and a rigid rotor system with wide-chord blades. Such improvements allowed the Charlie model to carry a wide range of weapon combinations. Most common were the minigun mated with various types of rocket launchers, and a nose-mounted 40mm grenade launcher. Although used in limited numbers, AGM-22B missiles appeared in Vietnam in late 1965 for use against hard targets, including armored vehicles. When North Vietnamese armor was encountered during early 1972, the experimental TOW (Tube-launched, Optically-tracked, Wire-guided) system was mounted to two UH-1Bs, which were quickly shipped to Vietnam. The pair would fire 101 TOW missiles, destroying 57 targets, including 24 tanks.

All Army Hueys in Vietnam flew with a crew of four: pilot, copilot, crew chief, and door gunner. Combat tactics varied according to unit policy and terrain, however, standard troop insertions with multiple Slicks and supporting gunships were called "Combat Assaults." The only U.S. Army Hueys assigned beyond Vietnam's borders, yet still involved with the war, belonged to the aviation section attached to the 46th Special Forces Company in Thailand. Throughout most of the Vietnam war, nearly every allied service in Southeast Asia would fly various versions of the popular Huey.

This seldom photographed view of an early Huey shows UH-1B (s/n 62-4589) at Nha Trang in 1964. The Huey wears high visibility markings, and is armed with 7-shot rocket launchers and M-60C machine guns. The yellow vertical lines on the fuselage are step guides. (Al Adcock)

A rocket-armed UH-1C of the 119th AHC gun platoon "Crocodiles" in 1967. An armor panel replaced the pilot's door window. Eyes were painted on the nose-mounted grenade launcher, the support braces of which are visible in the chin bubble. (Rodger D. Fetters)

UH-1Ds of the 1st Cavalry Division's 229th Assault Helicopter Battalion prepare for liftoff from a landing zone during the mid-1960s. The five companies within the battalion were assigned individual light blue geometric symbols worn on the pilots' doors. All wear the battalion "Winged Assault" emblem on the nose. (Bell Helicopter)

A blue square on a UH-1D Huey of the 1st Cavalry Division's 229th AHB identifies it as part of B Company, while the blue circle indicates an aircraft assigned to C Company in this 1965 photo. "Chalk," or position numbers in a flight, were applied to placards on Hueys' door posts. In the stowed position at the crew chief's position is the standard XM-23 system incorporating the M-60D machine gun. (Bell Helicopter)

Both miniguns of this Sharks UH-1C are fully depressed. In 1966 B/Gen (Ret.) Robert L. Scott, Jr. granted the 174th AHC permission to wear into battle the shark mouth worn by his P-40s of the 23rd Fighter Group in World War Two. (Fred Thompson)

The broad grins belong to UH-1Cs of the 174th AHC gun platoon named "Sharks." These two Hueys were part of a three-gunship heavy fire team on standby at Gia Vuc Special Forces Camp. (Fred Thompson)

A Huey crew chief points to damage from .51 cal. fire to a UH-1H of C Troop, 16th Cavalry "Darkhorse" in 1972. The geometric designator for the 13th Aviation Battalion is immediately forward of the orange synchronized elevators. (David Fesmire)

Fellow aircrew scramble to rescue the crew of this 176th AHC UH-1H after it was shot down near Binh Sonh in December 1968. The Huey lost tail rotor control after being hit by ground fire on a "sniffer" mission. (David Grieger)

UH-1Ds of A Company, 101st Aviation Battalion "Warriors" insert ground troops in 1965. (George Nonestied)

A UH-1B of the 120th AHC gun platoon "Razorbacks" in 1966. In keeping with the unit nickname "The Deans," a white mortarboard hat was painted on the nose immediately above the XM-5 grenade launcher. (Terry Love)

A gunship pilot makes an entry in the green logbook, which was carried on every Army aircraft during the war. In the foreground is this UH-1C's sliding armor for the pilot's seat. (Hugh Mills)

Double red roof bands identify this UH-1C as a Huey gunship belonging to the Air Cavalry Troop of the 11th Armored Cavalry Regiment in 1968. (John Griffith)

This UH-1D named "The Yellow Rose of Texas" belonged to the 121st AHC "Soc Trang Tigers" at Soc Trang in 1966. The Huey is armed with infantry type M-60A machine guns on early swivel mounts. (Lex McAulay)

"Eve of Destruction," a UH-1C of the 114th AHC gun platoon "Cobras," sits in a mortar-ravaged hangar at Vinh Long in late 1968. (Steve Huntley)

This Charlie of 7th Squadron, 17th Cavalry, based at Camp Enari, Pleiku, readies to fight PT-76 tanks near Dak To in 1968, (Robert N. Steinbrunn)

A trooper of the "Four Horsemen" Aero Rifle Platoon uses smoke and a colored panel to signal a Slick of D Troop, 1st Squadron, 4th Cavalry to pick up troops in July 1970. (Hugh Mills)

The SS-11 missile saw limited use in Vietnam, having first been used in combat in October 1965. The wire-guided missile had a range of 3,000 meters. The system seen here was mounted on a UH-1C of 7/17 "Ruthless Riders" in 1968. (Robert N. Steinbrunn)

The Huey helicopter became the enduring symbol of the Vietnam war, and this H model of the 92nd AHC "Stallions" in 1970 demonstrates the Huey's adaptability. (Rob Mignard)

The Huey continually exceeded its "utility" designation, this example, a UH-1H of the 71st AHC "Rattlers" utilized as a psywar "Bullshit Bomber." The bank of speakers mounted on the aircraft was easily removable, proving the Huey's versatility. Besides the white and yellow band signifying the parent 14th Combat Aviation Battalion, number 770 wore yellow trim on its tail boom. (Robert Brackenhoff)

The author photographed his gunner after an AK-47 round ripped through his helmet during a combat assault in 1971. That the gunner was unaware of his close call is evidence of strange occurrences in the heat of battle.

This Slick, s/n 67-17397, of the 176th AHC "Minutemen," was badly damaged when it flew over a demolition area in 1968. Huey units operating in northern regions wore black unit designators on pilot doors. (David Grieger)

Not all Huey losses were the result of combat. At An Khe in October 1965, the UH-1D (center) descended into the unsecured rotor blades of a UH-1B of the 2/20th ARA. (Ed Lemp)

With just enough room to land, this Slick of the 101st Airborne Division rests on the battle-scarred landscape of Fire Support Base Catherine. (Author's Collection)

"Ragin Cajun," a UH-1H of the 188th AHC, shows heavy battle damage. Ground attacks accounted for a large number of aircraft damaged or lost, a fact that highlights the importance of revetments. This UH-1H appears to have received a direct hit from a mortar or rocket. (Dick Detra)

This UH-1D of the 173rd AHC "Robin Hoods" at Lai Khe served Medal of Honor recipient Gary Wetzel. Wetzel was badly hurt when his slick took repeated rocket and machine gun hits near Can Giuoc on 8 January 1968. All 14 Hueys in the clash were damaged; three were shot down. (Gary Wetzel Collection)

A Troop D (Air), 1st Squadron, 4th Cavalry, 1st Infantry Division "Darkhorse" pilot waits in his UH-1D after an aero rifle platoon (ARP), the infantry element of an air cavalry unit, was inserted in late 1968. Freshly painted black and silver skids, long-line antennas on the belly, absence of door guns, and overall clean condition identify this Huey as a Command and Control aircraft, commonly called "C&C." (Hugh Mills)

"Peace maker" is a UH-1H of D Troop, 3rd Squadron, 4th Cavalry, 25th Infantry Division. A "chase ship" for recovery of downed aircrew in 1971, it packs a .50 cal. machine gun and twin M-60 machine guns in the opposite door. Its crew includes a medic and it carries a litter and Mk-24 flare dispenser. (Author)

A yellow bee adorns Slicks of the 116th AHC "Yellowjackets" lift platoon. This UH-1H at Duc Pho in 1970 carries a spray system powered by a port-side wind generator. (Robert Brackenhoff)

UH-1D "Rice Paddy Daddy" of the 56th Transportation Company recovers downed aircraft. On its doorpost is its impressive tally; "Good Nature" is painted on the nose. (Bell Helicopter)

A number of Army aviation units in Vietnam outfitted a Slick with a crew-operated minigun and powerful searchlight, mainly for base defense. The combination was called "Firefly" and was highly effective in countering night attacks. (Rob Mignard)

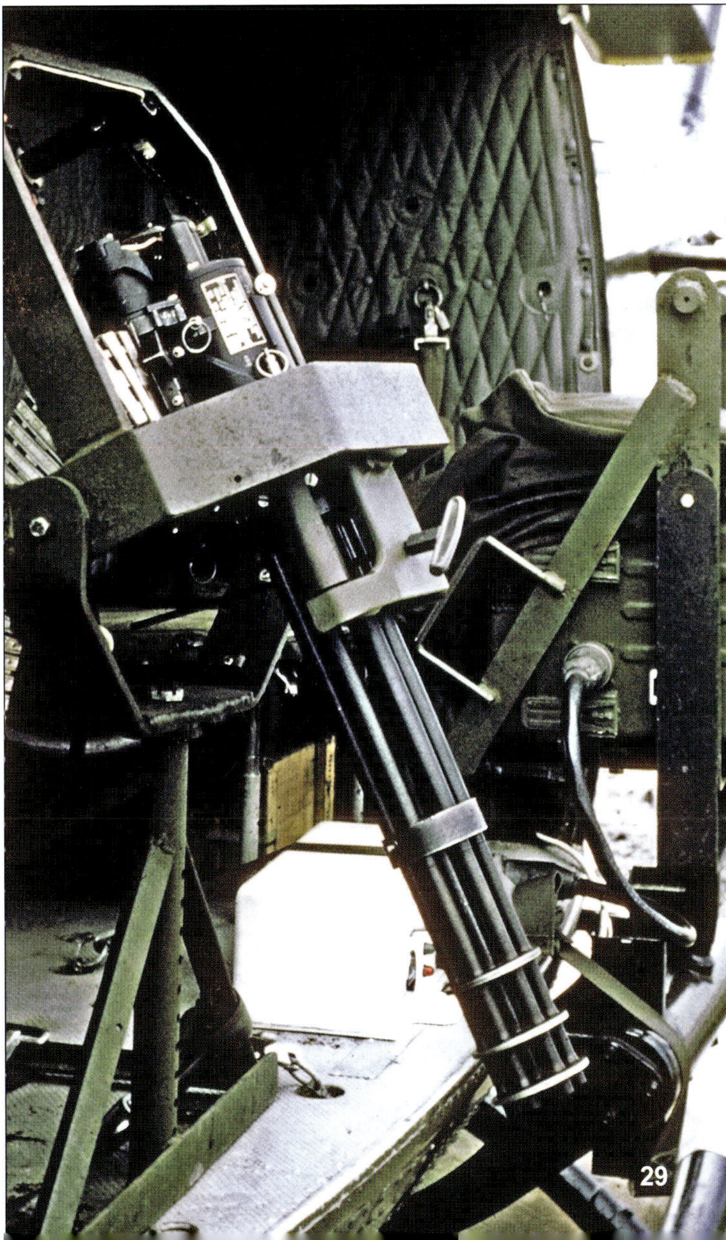

Hughes developed the TOW (Tube-launched, Optically-tracked, Wire-guided) missiles in 1970 and rushed them mounted on two UH-1Bs to Vietnam in April 1972 to counter North Vietnamese armor. Named the 1st Combat Aerial TOW Team, or "Hawk's Claw," the unit was effective against armor. (US Army)

One of two specially converted UH-1Bs of the 1st Combat TOW Team. Upturned engine exhausts helped protect the aircraft from heat-seeking SA-7 antiaircraft missiles. The TOW Hueys sported camouflage schemes like no other Army Hueys. (Bell Helicopter)

A 174th AHC "Dolphins" Slick (s/n 68-16340) air lifts infantry in 1970, when the Duc Pho-based unit served the 11th Light Infantry Brigade and 4th ARVN Regiment. Hueys rarely flew with cabin doors, and often omitted pilot doors too. (Don Alexander)

This 238th Aerial Weapons Company Huey UH-1B (s/n 63-12070) has the cambered tail fin of a UH-1C. Like most Army aviation in northern South Vietnam, the 238th "Gunrunners" put their unit mark on the pilot doors. M-60A machine guns are on swivel mounts, versus the popular cord-suspended "free 60." "Kill" markings are just forward of the wind baffle. (Larry D. Smith)

This UH-1M (s/n 65-9533) of the 176th AHC "Muskets" in 1971 is believed to be the last Huey gunship in Vietnam packing the XM-3 "Hog" rocket system. Wind baffles were often added to the forward edge of cabin door openings. (Craig Thoricht)

The 240th AHC gun platoon "Mad Dogs" posted slogans and a skull at the Camp Bearcat flight line operations shack. (Author)

UH-1C gunships of the 240th AHC "Mad Dogs" wore this elaborate nose art, which left no doubt about their work. Unusual is the absence of a black anti-glare nose, which accents the artwork on the avionics door. (Author's Collection)

The 269th Combat Aviation Battalion "Black Barons" located at Cu Chi was part of the 12th Combat Aviation Group. "Blackjack 6" was the call sign of the aircraft commander of this 269th CAB UH-1H. (Dick Detra)

Little was left to the imagination in this nose art version of Playboy character "Annie Fanny," on a UH-1H of Headquarters Company of the 1st Cavalry Division. (Author's Collection)

The buxom blonde caricature of Playboy fame, "Little Annie Fanny" was a favorite among soldiers in Vietnam. Accordingly, she adorned numerous aircraft in various poses. This UH-1H also wears the name "Stump Jumper," below which a scoreboard has been added. (Larry Davis Collection)

Little Annie Fanny shared the nose panel of 170th AHC Hueys with the emblem of the parent unit, the 52nd Combat Aviation Battalion, named "Flying Dragons." Annie wore either a red or blue bikini, depending upon the flight platoon. The First Flight Platoon was called "Bikini Blues." (Rodger D. Fetters)

"Sandra" was a UH-1H of the 1st Squadron, 9th Cavalry, 1st Cavalry Division in 1969. Yellow "X's" on the pilots' doors identified the squadron's Headquarters Troop. (Ray H. Janes)

This UH-1H of the 175th AHC "Outlaws" was based at Vinh Long in 1966. Its emblem refers to the 502nd Airmobile Infantry, which the unit supported. (George Nonestied)

One of the most lavishly painted aircraft of the 188th AHC was "Lucy in the Sky with Diamonds," a UH-1H (s/n 66-16119) painted in 1967 by gunner Dick Detra. (Dick Detra)

This door art on a UH-1H of the 188th AHC included an image of the satirical character Alfred E. Neuman. (Dick Detra)

A UH-1H of the 188th AHC. Army Huey units in Vietnam used between one and thee colored roof bands for unit identification. The 188th served only 13 months in Vietnam, at Bien Hoa AB, beginning in May 1967. (Dick Detra)

The 119th AHC evolved from the 81st Transportation Company, which flew CH-21s in Vietnam. "Gators" were the lift element of the 119th; the gun platoon were "Crocs." "The Flying Dragons" identified the parent command, the 52nd CAB. (John B. Hyde)

This Huey belongs to the 167th Transportation Detachment in Vietnam in 1965. (George Nonestied)

This is one version of the nose art emblazoned on Hueys of the 188th AHC "Black Widows." Although the Black Widows had one of the relatively shortest stays in Vietnam, the unit suffered severe combat casualties and numerous damaged aircraft. (Dick Detra)

The words "Flight To America" on the doors of this Slick were a clever means of displaying the letters "FTA," an abbreviation commonly used by Army personnel to convey an unsavory expression about the Army. The UH-1H, s/n 16221 of the 188th AHC, was destroyed at LZ Sally in June 1968. (Dick Detra)

"The D.B. III," which stood for "douche bag." was a UH-1B (s/n 64-14051) seen at Happy Valley during Operation Crazy Horse in May 1966. The red portion of the 1st Cavalry Division emblem signifies E battery, 82nd Artillery. (Ed Lemp)

"Miss Lou" is a UH-1B of the 114th AHC "Knights of the Air." Among the first units to fly the Huey in Vietnam, the 114th began its nine-year tour at Vinh Long in 1963. (George Nonestied)

"Scorpion 9" was a UH-1B of the 161st AHC. (Rick Davis)

The gun platoon of the 176th AHC "Muskets" based at Chu Lai used this nose art on its UH-1Cs. In keeping with helicopter unit bravado and much like motorcycle clubs of the period, crewmen of the 176th used the one-percent symbol to distinguish themselves as outcasts from normalized society. (Larry Davis Collection)

"Darkhorse" identified helicopters of C Troop, 16th Cavalry, 164th Combat Aviation Group, 1st Aviation Brigade. "Darkhorse 26" was the call sign of the aircraft commander of this UH-1H (s/n 70-15704) in 1972. It was common for Army aviation units in Vietnam to paint call signs on the aircraft. (David Fesmire)

"Free and Easy" was a UH-1H of 1st Flight Platoon "Bulldogs" of the 129th AHC. The "Cobras" were the 129th gun platoon The "Bite and Striker" Bulldog and Cobra platoons of the 129th worked throughout II Corps. The unit operated UH-1B, C, D, H, and M model Hueys, and the AH-1G. (Author's collection)

"Mystery Ship" of the 57th AHC. (J.W. Boyce)

This elaborate artwork adorned a Slick of the 57th AHC "Gladiators." The 57th, whose armed platoon was called "Cougars," was based at Kontum in the northern tri-border area where Vietnam, Laos, and Cambodia meet. Kontum often came under ground attack, inflicting heavy losses on the unit. (J.W. Boyce)

The 188th AHC "Black Widows" were particularly lavish with decoration. Door gunner Dick Detra on the UH-1C (s/n 66-15179) "Satisfaction," seen here in 1967, was also the artist. Black Widow gunships wore red trim; the 1st and 2nd lift platoons used yellow and white, respectively. In July 1968, when the 188th came under the 101st Aviation Battalion, all personal markings were banned much to the dismay of troops. (Dick Detra)

This UH-1B was flown by the 48th AHC "Jokers" in 1969. (Rob Mignard)

Heavy Lifters

Until the arrival in Vietnam of helicopters ideally suited for downed aircraft recovery, CH-21s performed the task. Each of the five CH-21-equipped transportation companies sent to Vietnam during 1962 had a Cargo Helicopter Field Maintenance (CHFM) detachment. Providing back-up to these detachments was the 339th Transportation Company, which had arrived in February. Since this Direct Support unit was based at Nha Trang in central Vietnam, units in southern delta regions were without heavy maintenance and recovery support. It wasn't until the 611th Transportation Company arrived at Vung Tau in October 1962, with a Beaver, an Otter, and a CH-21, that downed aircraft could be recovered in the Delta.

Providing the much needed heavy lift capability was A Flight, 1st Platoon, 19th Transportation Company, which introduced the Sikorsky CH-37B "Mojave" to Vietnam.

The unit traveled from Korea by ship, arriving at Saigon on 3 June 1963. Under operational control of the Army Concept Team in Vietnam, its four Mojaves were divided between the 339th and 611th Transportation Companies.

Able to lift 5,000 pounds, the Mojave could recover downed aircraft without major disassembly, hoisting with ease nearly intact CH-21s, and major Caribou components. This minimized time in the combat zone and subsequent re-assembly of aircraft. Since aircraft recovery often was contested by the enemy, Mojaves became known for their ability to withstand enemy fire. Nevertheless, one of the 19th's CH-37Bs was shot down during an aircraft recovery mission on 12 December 1963; four of its five crewmen were killed. The 19th TC was inactivated in early 1964, and in May, the 339th replaced its CH-21Cs with CH-37Bs. A third direct support unit, the 56th Transportation Company, began aircraft recovery operations with three CH-37Bs from Tan Son Nhut AB in October 1964.

In addition to supporting aviation units, the 339th in 1963 and 1964 often re-supplied Special Forces teams in the Central Highlands, and helped re-locate Montagnard villagers. One of the Mojaves was assigned at the request of the Air Force to Da Nang AB during late 1964 and early 1965. This aircraft flew in support of the classified mission code-named *Blue Spring*, which involved the use of various types of remotely piloted vehicles.

With the advent of the airmobile concept during the early 1960s, the Army sought a turbine-powered helicopter to replace its CH-21, CH-34, and CH-37. Boeing Vertol developed the HC-1B (later CH-47A) "Chinook," a large helicopter able to move troops and equipment within the combat zone. The tandem-rotor giant could carry more than five tons of cargo; eight tons on an external cargo hook. Load capabilities, however, were decreased in Vietnam's high density altitude.

Part of the 1st Cavalry Division's deployment to Vietnam in fall 1965 included the Chinook-equipped 228th Aviation Battalion. By year's end the 228th had recovered more than 100 downed aircraft. Although the Chinook was intended for assault troop transport in Vietnam, that role more often was filled by the UH-1 Huey. A primary mission of Chinooks was the emplacement and regular supply of artillery batteries atop mountain fire bases. The CH-47 proved to be dependable, highly adaptable to adverse weather conditions, and able to haul nearly anything, often under fire.

Chinooks in Vietnam were armed with M-60D machine guns at each side of the forward cabin; often cabin windows were removed allowing onboard troops to return fire. Beginning in 1967, some CH-47s mounted an M-60D or a .50 cal. Machine gun on the rear cargo ramp.

Boosting the Chinook inventory in Vietnam was the arrival of the first non-cavalry CH-47 unit in November 1965. Equipped with 18 CH-47As, the 147th Transportation Company began operations from Vung Tau. At the beginning of 1966, the 147th "Hillclimbers" was tasked with supporting the 1st and 25th Infantry Divisions, the 173rd Airborne Brigade, and Australian artillery. Next to arrive was the 178th "Boxcars," which went into business at Phu Loi, and in April began providing direct support from Chu Lai to *Task Force Oregon*, later known as the *Americal Division*. Like most Chinook units operating in Vietnam, the 178th was designated an Assault Support Helicopter Company (ASHC).

This CH-37B Mojave was one of the first four to serve in Vietnam, having arrived with A Flight, 1st Platoon, 19th Transportation Company in June 1963. It lifts a 57th TC CH-21C after it was shot down. The Mojave was a tremendous boost to the Army's recovery effort in Vietnam, and by October 1964, nine CH-37Bs were in country. (U.S. Army)

The CH-37B was one of the first Army aircraft in Vietnam to be painted in the low visibility scheme of overall Flat Olive Drab with black markings. This 56th Transportation Company CH-37B (s/n 57-1658) nicknamed "Wooly Bully," was shot down trying to recover a UH-1B on 23 September 1965. (B. Ellis)

At the start of 1968, the 178th received the first CH-47B model Chinooks, and by March, the first CH-47B unit was fully equipped. The CH-47B featured improvements in the airframe, rotor blades, and power plant that increased its external payload to nearly 10 tons. After 108 B models were produced for duty in Vietnam, the vastly improved CH-47C model followed early in 1968.

At the height of the war, 15 assault support helicopter companies were flying Chinooks in Vietnam, along with assault support helicopter battalions of the 1st Cavalry Division and the 101st Airborne Division, each having three CH-47 companies.

Transportation companies were assigned CH-47s mainly for aircraft recovery. Besides recovering aircraft and ground vehicles, hauling cargo, transporting troops, relocating villagers, and evacuating wounded, Chinooks functioned as bombers, usually against tunnel systems, dropping drums of napalm and tear gas. As expected, Air Force officials took a dim view of such infringement of their bombing role.

An even bigger thorn in the side of Air Force officials was a most unusual type of Chinook among the hundreds flying in Vietnam. Four A models of the 1st Cavalry Division's 53rd Aviation Detachment, nicknamed "Guns-A-Go-Go," had been extensively modified as the Army searched for a heavily armed support gunship.

Pending the arrival of Bell's Cobra gunship, the A/ACH-47A (*Armed and Armored CH-47A*) was powered by the CH-47B's more powerful T55-L-7 engines, and wore more than a ton of armor. Its crew comprised two pilots, a crew chief, and five gunners manning .50 cal. machine guns. A 40mm grenade launcher was fitted to the nose, and carried on stub wings were combinations of 20mm cannon, miniguns, and rocket launchers. A favorite of ground units, the tremendous firepower of the Guns-A-Go-Go allowed them to dominate every encounter with the enemy. Three of the A/ACH-47As were destroyed; two in combat, with the remaining aircraft returned to the U.S.

A total of 140 U.S. Army CH-47s were lost in Vietnam, 58 at the hands of the enemy. Of 15 ground combat losses, nine Chinooks were destroyed during an attack on Cu Chi on 26 February 1969.

King among the heavy lifters in Vietnam was Sikorsky's CH-54 "Tarhe," better known as the "Skycrane." Igor Sikorsky himself was the staunchest advocate of a flying crane, which, because of its

"How Sweet It Is" was a CH-37B, seen here with an M-60A machine gun on a modified Sagami mount in the cabin doorway. (Igor I. Sikorsky Historical Archives, Inc.)

unusual skeletal frame, could lift a 10-ton load. Of six prototype Tarhes ordered by the Army in June 1963, four became part of the 1st Cavalry Division's massive inventory shipped to Vietnam in fall 1965. The four YCH-54As formed the 478th Aviation Company (Heavy Helicopter), which provided support throughout I Corps. During its first three months in Vietnam, the 478th "Hurricanes" retrieved downed aircraft worth twice the cost of the four Tarhes. The Skycranes also proved their usefulness by lifting heavy artillery, bulldozers, trucks, and supplies.

Detachable pods, designed for use as command posts, troop transports, and mobile hospitals, were seldom used. In fact, the pod's four-point attachment system, along with more than 1,500 pounds of armor, were often removed to allow lift operations in Vietnam's high-dfdensity altitude.

In Vietnam the Skycrane flew with a crew of four: two pilots, a flight engineer, and mechanic. The latter pair occupied a rearward-facing station with pilot controls to handle load operations.

In December 1967 the 273rd Aviation Company (HH) arrived in Vietnam with eight Skycranes, operating from Long Binh's Sanford Airfield. To cover II Corps, the 355th Aviation Company (HH) began operations from Phu Hiep in January 1968. Eventually all three units had 10 CH-54s.

During the defense of Khe Sanh *(Operation Pegasus)* and related action in the A Shau Valley *(Operation Delaware)* in early 1968, CH54s set a record for tonnage carried. A total of 1,052 tons of engineering equipment, including trucks, bulldozers, and road graders, was moved in support of the two operations. To support battles in the A Shau Valley, the Skycranes lifted 103 155mm howitzers, weighing 710 tons, to mountain tops. The CH54s occasionally were pressed into service as bombers since they could carry a 10,000-pound bomb used to create instant landing zones, or decimate an area several hundred yards in diameter.

In 1969 the CH54As in Vietnam were joined by the heavier and more powerful CH54B. Featuring more powerful turbine engines and high-lift rotor blades, the B model could lift a 25-ton load. Although Chinooks became the Army's primary recovery vehicle in Vietnam, Skycranes remained until 1972, providing specialized heavy lift service. During eight years of combat operations, one CH-54 was shot down, while eight were lost to operational causes.

A CH-54 Tarhe lifts a Command and Control unit during Operation Masher at Bong Son Special Forces base in January 1966. During the operation, the CH-54 also carried the 155mm Howitzer, the first time the heavy artillery piece had been airlifted. (Ed Lemp)

The first-built YCH-54A (s/n 64-14202) was sent to Vietnam as part of its developmental trials. Here it lifts a UH-1D at An Khe, called "The Golf Course," in October 1965. (Ed Lemp)

CH-54A s/n 67-18414. Tail boom markings indicate the Skycrane's assignment to the 478th Heavy Helicopter Company, 101st Airborne Division. (Floyd Werner Collection)

The king of heavy lifters in Vietnam, the CH-54A Tarhe, better known as the "Skycrane," could lift nearly 12 tons, while the CH-54B could lift nearly 14 tons. This 1st Cavalry Division Skycrane, s/n 67-18416, prepares to lift a tower. The engine air particle separators over the aircraft's engines were developed by Sikorsky engineers in 1967 to contend with Vietnam's corrosive dust and sand. (Author's Collection)

"Slave Driver," a CH-37B supporting an artillery unit in Vietnam. (Igor I. Sikorsky Historical Archives, Inc.)

A weather-beaten CH-47B (s/n 67-18438) named "Good Vibrations" at Duc Pho in 1970. (Robert Brackenhoff)

Aircraft downed in enemy territory were hastily retrieved by recovery crews who often engaged in battle during operations. This Chinook crew obviously wasted no time in snatching a downed UH-1H of the 176th AHC in 1969. (David Grieger)

A CH-47A of the 179th Assault Support Helicopter Company, which was called both "Shrimpboats" and "Hooks." The Chinook's lower cabin door incorporated a boarding step. (Rodger D. Fetters)

Loaded with troops for Bob Hope's Christmas show, this CH-47 of the 228th Assault Support Helicopter Battalion lost a rotor blade on final to Phu Cat Air Base in 1967. The battalion was the 1st Cavalry's Chinook unit, which had three companies of 16 Chinooks each. (Ron Osburn)

This CH-47A of the 179th ASHC gets lots of attention from maintenance personnel at Camp Holloway, Pleiku in May 1967. Maintenance crews usually worked around the clock to keep aircraft availability rates high. (Rodger D. Fetters)

(Top) Cessna TO-1D of the 73rd Aviation Company (Airplane Surveillance Light). The 73rd "Warriors" was the first Army Bird Dog unit in Vietnam, having arrived in May 1963.

(Above) Beech RU-8Ds represented the largest number of fixed-wing aircraft used by the Army for signal intelligence in Southeast Asia. This example was assigned to the 146th Radio Research Company in 1970.

(Below) De Havilland U-1A 'Otters' flew a countrywide logistical network throughout the war.

(Bottom) Unique among the variety of Army aircraft in Vietnam was the Lockheed AP-2E "Neptune." Some were borrowed from Navy stocks for electronic intelligence work. The Neptunes were the heaviest aircraft the Army operated during the war.

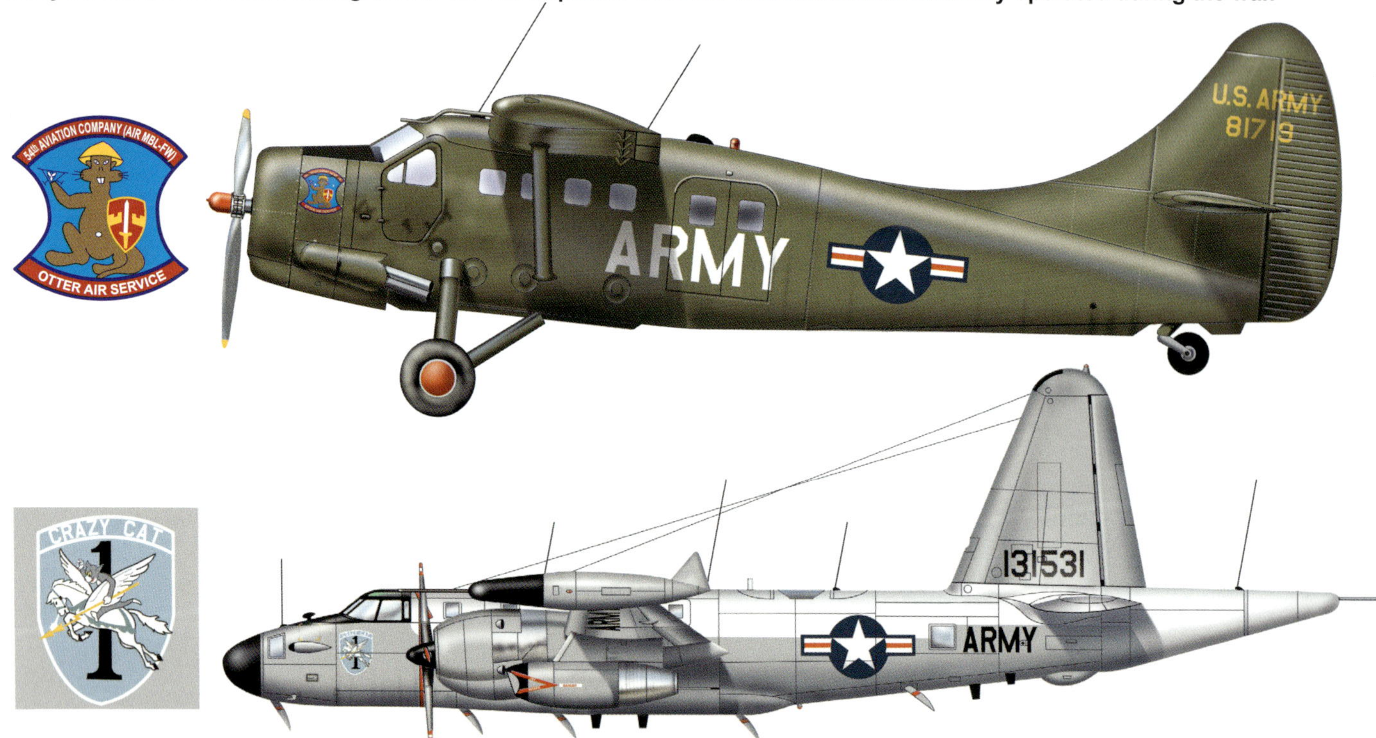

A CH-47B of the 101st Aviation Division prepares to sling-load fuel drums at Camp Eagle in 1969. The blunt trailing edge of the B model's rear rotor pylon was the most recognizable difference between it and the A model. (George Sullivan)

In its element, proving the versatility of helicopters and pilot skill, this CH-47B of the 196th ASHC "Flippers" eases into a tight mountaintop landing zone. Along with the blue flipper emblem, this Chinook wears the red, white and blue marking of the 17th Combat Aviation Group on its rear rotor pylon. (Author's Collection)

An extreme modification of the Chinook in Vietnam was the A/ACH-47A "Armed and Armored" version, of which four were built. The special aircraft satisfied the Army's search for a helicopter with massive firepower for support of ground troops. Serial number 64-13154 is seen here shortly after its arrival in Vietnam in May 1966. (Al Adcock)

A CH-47 Chinook (s/n 65-7984) of the 271st ASHC "Innkeepers" lands aboard Corpus Christi Bay in February 1971. The Innkeepers provided tactical and logistical airlift within IV Corps, better known as the Delta. Corpus Christi Bay was a floating aircraft maintenance facility tasked with depot-level maintenance. The vessel typically anchored three miles offshore of Vung Tau. (Stephen F. Foster)

Before the A/ACH-47A (s/n 64-13145) was named "Cost of Living," it bore the name "Crazy 8," which is barely visible forward of the cabin doorway. (Roy Benson)

A CH-54A in Vietnam demonstrates its lifting ability by sling-loading a damaged Navy F-4 Phantom. (Igor I. Sikorsky Historical Archives, Inc.)

The de Havillands

The rugged construction of aircraft built in Canada made them popular in the U.S. Army. Although their purchase for the U.S. military was strongly opposed by U.S. manufacturers, several fixed-wing types not only wore Army Olive Drab, but served in large numbers in Vietnam.

After World War II, de Havilland of Canada's (DHC) design team focused on the requirements for a rugged aircraft to serve the Canadian northlands. Work started on the DHC-2, which the company named the "Beaver," after Canada's bush pilots were canvassed for their perspective of the perfect bush airplane. Production began in 1947, with the first deliveries for the U.S. military beginning in 1951. The Beaver, which the Army initially designated C-137, and later L-20, was the first true STOL (Short takeoff and Landing) aircraft to go into large-scale production.

Beavers are believed to have been the first U.S. Army aircraft stationed in Vietnam. Two L-20s were assigned to the Flight Detachment of the Military Assistance Advisory Group at Saigon's Davis Station in October 1954. Painted in the high visibility red and white arctic scheme in the event they crashed into dense jungle, MAAG aircraft were strictly VIP transports. During 1961 and 1962 the detachment operated a float-equipped Beaver, which had the distinction of being the only Army float plane to serve in Vietnam.

Other Beavers that were early participants in the conflict were Radio Research conversions, and a U-6A assigned to the 611th Transportation Company in October 1962. Beavers eventually saw widespread use in Vietnam, with one or two commonly assigned to various units as utility aircraft.

Having achieved success with the Beaver, DHC engineers decided to design a "King Beaver," which would carry twice the payload but have the same performance. It too would be a single-engine, high-wing aircraft able to perform on wheels, skis, or floats. Production of the DHC-3, which was renamed the "Otter," began in 1951, with the first YU-1s delivered to the U.S. Army in 1955. The U.S. Army was the largest customer for the Otter, having purchased 190 examples.

The first Otters in Vietnam were two belonging to the 18th Airfield Operating Detachment, which set up shop at Soc Trang in October 1961. In February 1962 the Otter-equipped 18th Aviation Company arrived at Saigon aboard the *USNS Core*. The unit, whose motto was "Low, Slow, and Reliable," was headquartered at Nha Trang, but dispersed its Otters to best support Army Special Forces units and the four Corps regions. Otters quickly proved their value in support, becoming the main component of a utility network connecting widely spread units.

The 18th shouldered the load until the 54th Aviation Company and its Otters arrived in Vietnam in September 1965. With headquarters at Vung Tau, the 54th, whose nickname was "Big Daddy," operated a scheduled and on-call freight and passenger service throughout the III and IV Corps zones; the 18th covered the northern I and II Corps areas. Big Daddy Otters also flew combat re-supply missions, along with leaflet drops and photo-mapping missions. Although the newer and larger Chinook helicopter would have been the obvious choice for such work, the Otter was cheaper to operate and required less maintenance than any helicopter in the Army inventory.

The majority of Otters in Vietnam served with the 18th and 54th Aviation Companies, while others were assigned to the 2nd Signal Group, transportation companies, aviation battalions, and medical detachments. The first Radio Research conversions arrived in Vietnam during late 1967. The first Otter fatality in Vietnam occurred on 1 July 1963 when an 18th Avn. Co. U-1A crashed on takeoff from Hang Buc, killing the pilot. The following December another 18th U-1A was lost after departing Ban Me Thuot on a courier flight. Because it ran into rough weather or was shot down, the aircraft crashed into a mountain, its three-man crew becoming the first Otter combat loss.

A number of Otters were assigned to Military Assistance Command-Thailand, and in 1971, 19 Army U-1As were handed over to the Cambodian government.

"Snuffy" was a U-6A (s/n 58-2075) of Headquarters Detachment of the 2nd Signal Group in 1967. (Terry Love)

"Satisfaction" was a UH-1C gunship, which bore lavish personal markings familiar to the gun platoon of the 188th AHC in 1967.

Bell's OH-58A replaced the OH-6A in Vietnam for the Aeroscout mission. This "Kiowa" belonged to the Casper Aviation Platoon, Headquarters Company, 173rd Airborne Brigade. The Caspers, which supported the 173rd from 1965 to 1971, flew nine OH-58As beginning in 1970.

This rocket-armed AH-1G was an early model Cobra, which served the 7th Squadron, 1st Cavalry Regiment "Blackhawks."

This AH-1G (s/n 68-15201) was assigned to the AH-1G Training Team at Vung Tau, South Vietnam in 1969. It carries the standard weapons training load on both pylons: XM-18 minigun systems inboard, and XM-157 rocket launchers outboard.

The U-1A, s/n 58-1710, originally deployed to Vietnam with the 18th Aviation Company in January 1962, was returned to the U.S. for overhaul, then went back to Vietnam with HHD, 2nd Signal Group. Named "Handy Capp," it was one of two Otters assigned, the other being 59-2225, named "Red Baron." (Terry Love)

Since de Havilland's arctic and bush airplane designs meshed closely with Army requirements, the bond between them grew stronger. Intending to expand their aviation support branch, Army planners again went to de Havilland, this time seeking a fixed-wing transport that featured the proven STOL performance of the Beaver and Otter. It was also to have the load-carrying ability of the CH-47 Chinook, with which it was to be fielded. The result was the DHC-4, which the Army labeled the YAC-1 "Caribou." Deliveries to the Army began in 1961, and in August 1961, a single Caribou was sent to Vietnam for troop carrier tests. A total of 56 AC-1s, which were re-designated CV-2As, were built, followed by 103 CV-2Bs, which featured structural changes, allowing a gross weight of 28,500 pounds.

Initial requests by the Army to deploy a Caribou unit to the war zone were turned down, but then in April 1962, Defense Secretary Robert McNamara directed Army leaders to come up with ways to increase troop mobility in Vietnam. The result was the delivery of Caribous of the 1st Aviation Company to Thailand in June 1962. The following month, eight of the Caribous were relocated to Vietnam and dispersed to Da Nang, Nha Trang, and Tan Son Nhut

This crashed U-1A of the 18th Aviation Company wears the red, white, and blue markings of the 17th Combat Aviation Group on its tail. (Larry Wagoner)

to provide support in each Corps area. Ten more Caribous arrived in December that year.

Despite Air Force opposition, the 61st Aviation Company deployed to Vung Tau in July 1963 and joined 1st Aviation Company in flying support missions throughout Vietnam. After 1st Aviation Company Caribous were modified in 1963 with reversible pitch propellers, they were able to operate from 15 airfields that had previously been unusable during the rainy season. The addition of nose-mounted weather avoidance radar also improved Caribou operations.

The 1st Aviation Company withdrew from Vietnam in December 1963 as part of a token troop reduction, but five Caribou units would later be sent to Vietnam. The 92nd Aviation Company arrived in November 1964 with 16 Caribous, and in September 1965 the 17th Avn. Co. began supporting the 1st Cavalry Division at An Khe. At General William Westmoreland's request, the Caribou-equipped 57th, 134th, and 135th Aviation Companies deployed to Vietnam in December 1965. The 57th became the third U.S. Army Caribou unit based at Vung Tau, while the 134th went to Can Tho, and the 135th to Dong Ba Thinh.

Early in the war, Caribous were popular with Special Forces teams, which relied on airdropped supplies. Such missions were high-risk for Caribou crews since approaches to remote outposts were dangerous, as were the steep climb-outs. Loads were dropped by parachute, or using the Low Level Extraction (LOLEX) method, in which a deployed parachute pulled palletized cargo out of the cargo compartment as the aircraft skimmed the ground. Thanks to its superior STOL characteristics, the Caribou outperformed Air Force C-123 and C-130 aircraft in operations at small strips.

When the Army/Air Force feud over tactical airlift responsibility came to a head, the Army relinquished most of its Caribou assets to the Air Force. Under *Operation Red Leaf*, the transfer of 144 CV-2s was complete by January 1967. Air Force *Bou* crews flew basically the same missions that the Army had performed. Some Caribous also passed to the South Vietnamese Air Force beginning in 1971. Meanwhile, the CIA's air arm, *Air America*, flew Caribous in Vietnam, as did the Vung Tau-based Royal Australian Air Force Caribou Flight, later called No. 35 Squadron, mainly in support of the Australian Task Force.

Increasing demand for Caribous in Vietnam prompted Army leaders in 1962 to solicit proposals for a larger, turbine-powered version of the Caribou. Having wisely anticipated the Army's needs, de Havilland had modified a Caribou test-bed with turboprop engines. Impressed with the results, the Army selected the DHC-5 "Buffalo," which later became the CV-7A. The Buffalo obviously was a direct descendant of the Caribou with the exception of its "T" tail. The CV-7A could carry nearly twice the load of the Caribou, yet its high-lift wing with double-slotted flaps and spoilers gave it STOL performance surpassing the Caribou. In spring 1965 four prototypes were delivered to the U.S. Army, two of which were sent to Vietnam for a three-month evaluation beginning in November. The pair was assigned to the 92nd Aviation Company at Nha Trang, flying support for Special Forces. Unfortunately for the Army, the Buffalos were classified under the 1966 Army/Air Force agreement regarding large fixed-wing transport aircraft, and they too were transferred to the Air Force.

Thirty-one Army and Air Force Caribou crewmen lost their lives during the Vietnam conflict, along with 20 aircraft.

The Army's U-6A Beaver was one of the first aircraft converted from a utility role to that of intelligence gathering. The Beaver's special receiver gear homed in on signals emitted by enemy transmitters. Along with white-painted upper surfaces to protect sensitive equipment from solar heat, this RU-6A of the 146th Radio Research Company wore the popular Snoopy character on its engine cowl in 1970. (John B. Hyde)

To strengthen America's position in Thailand, the U.S. Army buildup began in May 1962 with the establishment of the U.S. Military Assistance Command in Thailand. Among the aircraft supporting Army operations in Thailand in 1970 was this weary U-1A Otter. The majority of U.S. Army aircraft stationed in Thailand were assigned to the 46th Aviation Company. (Mark Eyestone)

A CV-2B Caribou of the 57th Aviation Company "Gray Tiger Lines," offloads troops and equipment at LZ X-Ray in the Ia Drang Valley in late 1965. Since transport aircraft were fat targets for enemy gunners, engines were kept running to facilitate hasty departures. (Sidney Reeder)

A plug-in boom hoist is used to remove a damaged engine from this CV-2A Caribou, while its replacement is inspected. The engine swap took place at Ban Me Thuot, a remote forward operating base. The Caribou is s/n 61-2404 of the 1st Flight Platoon "Blue Diamonds," 61st Aviation Company, which deployed to Vietnam with 18 Caribous in 1963. (Al Adcock)

This CV-2A (s/n 61-2388) of the 1st Aviation Company crashed in Thailand during August 1963, prior to the unit's deployment to Vietnam. (U.S. Army)

Few photographs exist showing de Havilland's Buffalo in Vietnam, since only two aircraft spent only three months undergoing combat evaluation. Here, one of the pair, s/n 63-13689, prepares to depart Pleiku in December 1965. (Ed Lemp)

Dust Off

In the history of warfare, nothing has meant hope for survival more than the words "Dust Off," the term synonymous with medical evacuation (medevac) by helicopter. Soldiers serving in the Vietnam war felt some measure of comfort knowing that if they were wounded, a dedicated helicopter crew would make every effort to pull them from the battlefield. It has been said that a person's chance of survival was greater if he were wounded on a battlefield in Vietnam than if he were injured in an auto accident on a highway in the United States. From 1962 to 1973 U.S. Army Dust Off crews flew nearly half a million missions in Vietnam, evacuating more than 900,000 persons, resulting in a death rate of less than one percent among casualties who survived the first 24 hours. But such impressive statistics were not without a high price; Dust Off was three times more dangerous than other helicopter missions.

Prior to the establishment of organized medical evacuation in Vietnam, the small number of U.S. aircraft in the theater performed such services. As the tempo of operations and the number of troops and aircraft increased, the 57th Medical Detachment (Helicopter Ambulance) was sent to Vietnam. During late April 1962, elements of the 57th began arriving at the coastal base Nha Trang, where the 8th Field Hospital had been established just months earlier. Since more action was taking place farther north and south, two of the 57th's HU-1As were sent to Qui Nhon to support northern combat operations.

Not only did the 57th bring the first Huey helicopters to Vietnam, its personnel were the first to use the name "Huey." Don Lidstone, who served as a crew chief with the 57th Med. Det. at Fort Meade, Maryland, states, "I remember when we first called our A models 'Hueys' because the Army-assigned name 'Iroquois' did not seem too popular, and it didn't catch on with men in our unit." Some of the first HU-1As off the production line went to medical evacuation units to replace Sikorsky H-19 helicopter ambulances. Beginning in 1959, the 57th received five HU-1As, having constructor numbers 22 through 26.

The first casualty picked up by the 57th was a wounded Vietnamese soldier, despite a command directive that the unit not evacuate Vietnamese. Such restrictions would soon be ignored. Business was slow and the unit's importance went largely unrecognized. That especially became evident when Hueys arrived for other units, creating a logistical nightmare. When those units became plagued with faulty starter generators, the 57th was ordered to relinquish theirs to keep lift companies up to strength. That grounded the 57th until the unit's commander, Capt. John Temperelli, convinced the Army Support Group to keep one Huey flyable in the Nha Trang area.

The decisive battle at Ap Bac on 2 January 1963, during which allied forces sustained heavy troop and aircraft losses, played a large part in the decision to relocate the 57th in mid-January to Tan Son Nhut Air Base, Saigon, placing it closer to the action. Still, the unit's efforts were countered by commanders who argued against dedicating aircraft for medical evacuation. Many insisted that all aircraft carry removable red crosses, allowing them to fly medevac missions. Some felt that air ambulance companies should be transferred from the Medical Corps to the Transportation Corps, which governed Army air operations in Vietnam. Despite

The 57th Medical Detachment (Helicopter Ambulance) brought the first Hueys to Vietnam. Seen shortly after its arrival at Nha Trang in May 1962 is s/n 58-2081, one of five UH-1As flown by the 57th. This Huey was the 13th A model off the production line, having constructor number 22. (Bill Hardy)

Chuck Lawhorn, door gunner, wearing "chicken plate" armor with a Superman emblem, poses with a UH-1H of Air Ambulance Platoon, 15th Medical Battalion, 1st Cavalry Division in Vietnam 1971. Unusual is the absence of the Huey's standard flat black anti-glare nose. (Author's Collection)

This pair of UH-1Ds of the 254th Medical Company at Tan Son Nhut in November 1966 attest to the high risk nature of Dust Off missions in Vietnam. (Terry Love)

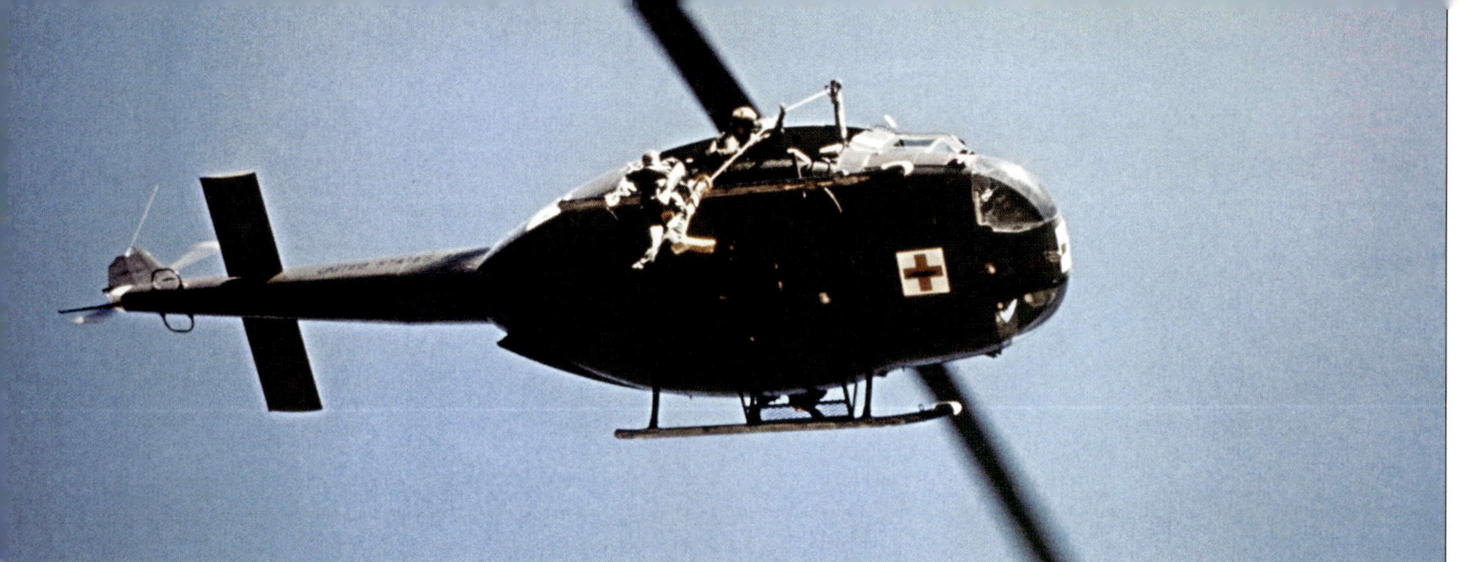

UH-1H of the 57th Med uses its jungle penetrator hoist to evacuate a trooper of the 16th Cavalry Aero Rifle Platoon from the Iron Triangle. (Hugh Mills)

This UH-1H of the 159th Medical Detachment rests on the bow pad of USS Corpus Christi Bay in Vung Tau Harbor. The Huey wore its name "Lord of the Flies" on the cabin auxiliary doors (Bruce Nelson)

This UH-1H (s/n 69-15360) of the 159th Med. Co. is loaded with hoists for rebuild aboard Corpus Christi Bay in early 1971. (Bruce Nelson)

such opposition, the 57th managed to keep pace with an increase in fighting, often shifting its aircraft and crews from one site to another. By the end of March the unit had replaced its UH-1As with B models, and in April it established a two-aircraft detachment at Pleiku in the Central Highlands to support Special Forces and the 52nd Aviation Battalion. Ground commanders were better able to utilize medevac helicopters after the 57th acquired the call sign "Dust Off" and its own permanent radio frequency. By the end of 1963 the 57th Medical Detachment had evacuated 1,825 Vietnamese and 157 Americans.

Since the 57th was hard-pressed to maintain its goal of having Dust Off choppers available in 15 minutes anywhere in South Vietnam, combat helicopter crews often evacuated wounded. One unit made an extra effort to fill the void. After the 117th Aviation Company was activated in June 1963 at Quin Nhon from the 8th Transportation Company, some of its officers formed a search and rescue team. Under the command of Lt. Laurence Walker, the team comprised about 20 volunteers who were specially trained for rescues in all terrain. A typical rescue for the SAR team involved rappelling from a Huey, setting up a defensive perimeter, rendering medical attention, clearing a landing zone for the rescue chopper, and staying with the downed aircraft until it was recovered.

During January 1964, Major Charles Kelly took command of the 57th Medical Detachment. Kelly would become a legend not only for his fierce dedication to the Dust Off mission, but for defending the unit's very existence from bureaucracy. Although at that time in the war, helicopter operations ceased at nightfall, Kelly did not consider the darkness a barrier. As proof, after moving his detachment to Soc Trang, he and his crew regularly flew an extensive course over the delta, letting ground units know he was available to evacuate wounded. On many nights, Kelly evacuated more than a dozen patients, some of whom otherwise would have died. Such missions became so routine that transponders were installed in the 57th's Hueys, enabling pilots to work with Air Force radar at Can Tho. Dust Off crews were inspired by Kelly to fly every mission and not leave until they had the wounded aboard. Kelly rotated his men for the dangerous night missions, but kept his name at the top of the flight roster, flying more missions than his men. Some pilots stopped logging excess hours for fear the Flight Surgeon would ground them. Enhancing Kelly's spirited reputation was his battle with the Surgeon General's office over his belief that medevac pilots remain assigned to the Medical Service Corps. Even prior to

For reasons that defy explanation, the Army Medical Command in Vietnam in 1971 ordered that all medevac Hueys be painted white. The first example appeared in October and eventually most were shot down. (Author)

the war's onset, medevac pilots received medical training at Brooke Army Medical Center, Fort Sam Houston, Texas. Besides the pilots, Dust Off crews comprised a crew chief and medic, who were cross-trained in each other's duties.

Kelly had evacuated some 500 casualties since his arrival in Vietnam, when on 1 July 1964, he and his crew were called out again to evacuate wounded. As Kelly hovered over the rice paddy, the enemy began firing, prompting the ground advisor to radio, "Get out, Dust Off. Get out!" Immediately after calmly responding, "Not until I have your wounded," a bullet pierced Kelly's heart. The UH-1B, serial number 63-08591, rolled over and was destroyed, but the other three crewmen survived. Kelly's conviction cost him his life, but it also erased the question of whether dedicated medevac helicopters were needed.

Accordingly, in 1964, five more medical detachments received orders for Vietnam. First among them to be deployed was the 82nd Medical Detachment, which set up shop in November with five UH-1Bs at Soc Trang to cover IV Corps. That allowed the 57th to concentrate on the III Corps area. Although the 57th provided training, the 82nd's commander, Major Henry Capozzi, put an end to flying night circuits over the delta.

The remaining four units arrived during 1965; the 283rd and 254th Medical Detachments, with six Hueys each, and the 498th Medical Company, with 25 aircraft, which were divided into four platoons to cover II Corps. Part of the 1st Cavalry Division's massive deployment to Vietnam in September 1965 included an air ambulance platoon of the 15th Medical Battalion. Equipped with 12 UH-1Ds, this unit broke from the tradition of using the Dust Off call sign, using "Medevac" instead. The month-long campaign known as the Battle of the Ia Drang Valley proved the value of the Cav's air ambulances. This unit was unique in that four of its Hueys were equipped for crash rescue.

Although units in Vietnam received the highest priority, a shortage of aircraft and Medical Service Corps pilots continued to plague the medevac organization. More units arrived and by 1966, all but two were flying UH-1Ds. By 1967, medevac had grown into an organized mission, complete with operational guidelines and full support from senior commanders. Its primary mission of evacuating all injured persons, regardless of nationality, was backed by a secondary mission of transporting whole blood and key medical personnel. The dead were transported if it did not interfere with saving lives. Geneva Convention restrictions on hauling ammunition were periodically ignored by air crews who reasoned that it was better than later hauling out soldiers killed or wounded as a result of having depleted their ammunition. Similar rules regarding defensive armament were side-stepped. Personal weapons were abundant for "patient protection," with Dust Off crews often fighting their way into and out of landing zones. The air ambulance platoon of the 1st Cavalry was the major exception, having mounted M-60 machine guns to their Hueys.

Although medevac Hueys were forbidden to make pickups in areas declared too "hot" without gunship protection, they usually went in anyway, as gunship protection often was either unavailable, or waiting for it meant losing precious minutes for the wounded. Bruce Terry, who was a Dust Off pilot with the 571st Med. Det. during 1967 and 1968, adds, "Eighty percent of our missions were flown without gunship protection or any kind of escort. We were forbidden from going into any LZ without them. Nobody ever paid attention to that; if we had, we'd never have gotten anyone out." Many Dust Off pilots felt it was what Chuck Kelly would have done. Having Kelly's ghost riding in the right front seat of their choppers bolstered the determination of many Dust Off pilots to the extent that they competed for missions, a practice that came to be called "scarfing." Approaches to a pickup site were made either low and

The jungle penetrator, which featured three fold-down arms to form a seat, found favor with Army and Air Force helicopter crews. It is seen here in its standard location on Army Hueys, the right forward cabin area. Credit for its basic design goes to the Navy, whose helicopter rescue forces first used the device a decade earlier. (U.S. Army)

Dust Off crews did not discriminate. Despite the fact that enemy gunners ignored the internationally recognized red cross, Dust Off crews evacuated thousands of enemy soldiers. Here, soldiers of Company A, 124th Signal Battalion load a wounded Viet Cong soldier on a Huey during Operation Clean Sweep in October 1968. His M-16 at the ready, the Huey crew chief watches intently. (U.S. Navy)

Litters were first used for medevac in 1966. Although often ineffective in jungle terrain, they provided this wounded soldier a comfortable ride to the deck of a Navy ship from a UH-1H of the 571st Medical Detachment. Major Vince Cedola, who commanded the 571st from November 1967 to November 1968, changed the white field of the red cross to a white outline. (Bell Helicopter)

fast, or in a spiral descent, in which a chopper literally dropped from a few thousand feet altitude. In the LZ, pilots preferred to point the aircraft's tail toward the enemy, not only to set up for departure, but because that placed more of the aircraft between them and the enemy. Still, night and weather claimed more Dust Off crewmen than the enemy.

With the increase in the number of medevac units, in March 1966 the 44th Medical Brigade assumed control of most medevac units in Vietnam. Subordinate to the Brigade were Medical Groups responsible for each Corps area. Beginning in September 1966 medevac Hueys were fit with rescue hoists. Mounted behind the co-pilot's seat, the hoist boom rotated 90 degrees, and its electrically-powered winch could lift 600 pounds on a 256-foot cable. After litters used with the hoist proved ineffective in jungle terrain, a forest penetrator was introduced. The device had three spring-loaded arms that folded alongside the tapered hoist body. Bruce Terry states, "The most hazardous missions that I ever experienced were hoist missions. They were real killers. There were all kinds of hazards associated with them, one of them being that you were a stationary target, sitting on top of 200 gallons of JP4, with no way to autorotate at that high of a hover. An engine failure or getting hit with a B40 rocket in a hover would prove disastrous, not only for the crew but the casualty on the hoist and whoever was on the ground because we would come down in a ball of flames. There were cases where guys dropped the jungle penetrator down through the thick canopy and the ground troops couldn't find it. Worse, they would get it stuck in the trees and we'd have to cut it off. Or you'd try to hoist an ARVN and there were four or five of his buddies with him. You try to pull them up and you can't do it. You cut 'em off or you're going down. The boys up north had it worse than we did and had to use the hoist more. At least we had paddies sometimes."

In October 1967 the 50th Medical Detachment of the 101st Airborne Division arrived in Vietnam, setting up shop at Tuy Hoa with six factory-fresh UH-1Hs. Shortly before becoming the Air Ambulance Platoon of the 326th Medical Battalion of the 101st, the 50th chose the call sign "Eagle Dust Off." Although four of the unit's additional UH-1Hs were to be crash rescue aircraft, none were rigged as such. All 12 aircraft, however, were equipped with a large fire extinguisher and a hoist. No door gunners were carried, providing more room and weight allowances for patients.

By 1968, 110 medevac Hueys were evacuating about 8,000 casualties per month. The Tet Offensive during January 1968 put Dust Off to the test. More than 8,000 wounded were evacuated during this 12-day period, during which 40 of 64 operational medevac Hueys were hit by enemy fire. The need for more medevac helicopters was obvious, and by August the organization peaked with the addition of four detachments sent to Vietnam. By year's end, all medevac units were equipped with UH-1H model Hueys.

A dramatic increase in 1969 to 18,000 casualties evacuated per month was attributed to an increase in the number of Hueys to 140, plus a greater number of Vietnamese Dust Off missions. Casualties in Vietnam were not picked up at aid stations, but at the site where they received their injuries. Often patients were backhauled by medevac helicopters to other treatment facilities. At the war's peak, medevac crews were flying casualties to 17 Field, Surgical, and Evacuation hospitals throughout South Vietnam, along with two hospital ships, the *USS Repose* (AH-16) and the *USS Sanctuary* (AH-17).

Medical Evacuation Helicopter Units in Vietnam
(in order of arrival)

57th Medical Detachment
82nd Medical Detachment
Air Ambulance Platoon,
15th Medical Battalion, 1st Cavalry Division
283rd Medical Detachment
498th Medical Company
254th Medical Detachment
436th Medical Company, later 658th Medical Company
45th Medical Company
54th Medical Detachment
326th Medical Battalion, 101st Airborne Division
159th Medical Detachment
236th Medical Detachment
571st Medical Detachment
50th Medical Detachment,
later Air Ambulance Platoon, 326th Medical Battalion
237th Medical Detachment
68th Medical Detachment
247th Medical Detachment
Long Binh Dust Off
215th Composite Service Battalion (Support)
1st Cavalry Division

Unable to land, a UH-1H Dust Off crew takes on casualties of 4th Battalion, 173rd Airborne Brigade, who fought at Hill 875 near Dak To in November 1967. (U.S. Army)

Soldiers of the 25th Infantry Division's 6th Armor place a wounded comrade aboard a 1st Cavalry Division UH-1D in March 1966. Medevac Hueys of the 1st Cav were the exception to the policies of armed medical evacuation aircraft. In the absence of visible gun mounts, this Huey crew used M-60As suspended from straps. (U.S. Army)

Considering the high-risk nature of Dust Off, it came as no surprise that three Dust Off crewmen were awarded the Medal of Honor. The first went to Major Patrick Brady, who, in a single day on 5 January 1968, navigated through heavy fog and gunfire during numerous missions to save 51 seriously wounded, often trading his shot-up Huey and wounded crewmen for fresh ones. On 2 October 1969, Dust Off pilot Chief Warrant Officer Michael Novosel of the 82nd Med. Det. and his crew made repeated approaches during 11 hours of flying to rescue 29 wounded soldiers pinned down by heavy enemy fire. Then, during the fierce battles of the Cambodian incursion in Spring 1970, SFC. Louis Rocco, aboard a Huey of the 1st Cav's Air Ambulance Platoon, although seriously wounded, rescued others before allowing himself to be rescued by Dust Off.

Dust Off crews had to land in some of the most difficult terrain imaginable, and often under fire. Sometimes, as seen here, rough terrain ruled out landings. (Bell Helicopter)

Although one VNAF medevac helicopter squadron was reported formed in 1974, this VNAF UH-1H (s/n 67-17627) and others similarly marked, were assigned to "Long Binh Dust Off" in 1971. The Huey has an M-60 door gun mount. (Bruce Nelson)

In 1971 the 159th and 283rd detachments combined to form *Long Binh Dust Off.* This was also the year the Army Medical Command in Vietnam decided that painting medevac helicopters overall white would reduce their losses. How wrong they were. The scheme did little except to make them an even better target. Regardless, all medevac Hueys were painted white. In conjunction with the new paint scheme, all armament was removed, gunship escort was eliminated, and documents explaining the mercy mission of white Hueys were rained upon the countryside. The only noticeable response from the enemy was an increase in ground fire, including heat-seeking missiles introduced in April 1972. Although March 1971 marked the end of duties of most of the 1st Cavalry Division, in June remnants formed the 215th Composite Service Battalion (Support), which included a flight of six medevac Hueys stationed at Bien Hoa AB. The U.S.-supported medevac organization also spawned *Project Whitehorse,* begun in January 1973, which involved nine U.S. Army UH-1M Hueys used for medevac in Laos, but flown by Thai Army volunteers.

On 11 March 1973, the 57th, appropriately, flew the last U.S. Dust Off mission in Vietnam. Like most military operations, the Dust Off role was passed to the South Vietnamese Air Force. Reportedly, the only VNAF medevac unit was the 259th Helicopter Squadron, formed during late 1974. This was the VNAF's last helicopter unit formed, consisting of eight detachments of eight to 12 Hueys, which operated from major air bases throughout South Vietnam. Although the 259th is officially reported as having been the only VNAF medevac unit, VNAF UH-1Hs wearing medevac markings were assigned to Long Binh Dust Off in 1971.

Vincent Cedola, Dust Off pilot with the 82nd Med. Det. during 1964 and 1965, and later the 571st, explains aircraft markings: "At Soc Trang we noticed that many of the gunshot hits to flying helicopters were aft of the cabin. This told us that *Charlie* was not leading the shot, but aiming directly at the bird. To help them miss, some units painted the bottom of the horizontal stabilizers white and some painted large eyeballs. This was fine until captured enemy documents revealed a crude stick figure sketch showing a soldier pointing his rifle at a helicopter with a dotted line aimed in front of the bird. Charlie learned how to duck-shoot."

The traditional markings for Dust Off was a large white square with a bright red cross centered. The markings were on the roof, nose, both cabin doors and belly. Our first modification was to paint out the belly markings, which was too much of a target. At Phu Bai, to cut down some of the bright white and to add a distinctive touch to the 571st, I simply outlined the red crosses on the nose and doors. We left the large marking on the roof to aid in identification when we were on the ground. The 1st Cav removed the white and had dull red crosses on Olive Drab." Some units painted portions of the cabin roof area of their Hueys white, and some had the words "Ambulance" or "Dust Off" in white on cabin doors or windows.

During 11 years of Dust Off operations in Vietnam, 211 crewmen were killed and many more were wounded. The Dust Off experience and tradition continue, with Army pilots and crews performing life-saving operations in the U.S. and abroad, in combat. To the injured, the large red cross of an Army helicopter remains one of the most beautiful sights.

Aeroscouts

In October 1958 the Army's Research and Development office began work on a study aimed at improving various aspects of Army Aviation. One of the studies called for light observation helicopters to replace the Korean war vintage L-19 Bird Dog, along with the Hiller OH-23 and Bell OH-13 piston-powered helicopters. The new turbine-powered helicopter was envisioned as an aerial equivalent of the famed jeep, a minimum-sized vehicle capable of performing a variety of missions. From a storm of controversy, politics and corporate rivalry emerged the Hughes OH-6A "Loach," a nickname derived from the abbreviation *LOH*, for *Light Observation Helicopter*. More than 1,400 Loaches were built for the U.S. Army, more than half of which were lost in Vietnam.

The OH-6A went to war in the hands of bawdy, but highly effective, crewmen known as "Aeroscouts." This tenacious and courageous bunch were usually volunteers, as they were often outgunned and regularly engaged in close-quarter combat. Constantly facing death, they relied heavily on each other, with their camaraderie and bravado becoming the substance of legend. The enemy found this fierce breed a force to be reckoned with. Aeroscouts were a major component in air cavalry troops, airmobile divisions, and infantry divisions, each of which had an aeroscout troop or squadron authorized nine scout helicopters.

Early aeroscout units in Vietnam flew OH-13S "Sioux" and OH-23G "Raven" helicopters for aerial reconnaissance. Both had been frontline Army observation aircraft, however, their performance was limited in Vietnam's high density altitude. Although underpowered for the scout mission, they pioneered the air cavalry concept. When the 11th Air Assault Division became the 1st Cavalry Division in late 1965, the 11th AAD's 3rd Squadron, 17th Air Cavalry, which had been formed in March 1964, became 1st Squadron, 9th Cavalry. This squadron would fly the OH-13S in Vietnam for two years before receiving OH-6As. In the meantime the OH-6A New Equipment Training Team (NETT) had arrived with two aircraft in February 1967. Slow production of the OH-6A prompted Army leaders to transfer 71 OH-13Ss from Europe and 43 OH-23Gs from Korea to Vietnam to meet observation requirements. Although three Loach-equipped air cavalry units had arrived in Vietnam by the end of 1967, and nearly 90 OH-6As had been deployed, that was far short of the 377 the Army hoped to have in the theater. In January 1968, when the decision was made to convert the 101st Airborne Division to an airmobile force, 30 OH-6As were rushed to Vietnam by the end of February. By the end of 1968 there were 542 OH-6As in Vietnam, despite losses that already totaled 208 aircraft. Although OH-6A losses were high, the Army maintained between 540 and 590 OH-6As in Vietnam through peak war years.

While U.S. infantry divisions were in Vietnam, air cavalry squadrons were under their operational control. As more Loaches arrived to serve as reconnaissance elements, tactics were developed. Scout crews learned quickly that to find the enemy they had to fly not only above the trees, but often below them, facing the enemy mere feet away. Although tactics varied according to terrain and unit policy, some basic concepts were adopted.

The most widely used tactic had Loaches working as a two-ship team; one high and one low. The low bird prowled in the enemies' backyard, while the high bird watched protectively, providing navigation by radio. When contact with the enemy was made, the scout snapped clear, allowing orbiting gunships to roll in on the target. If a substantial target was encountered, the aerorifle platoon was airlifted to the battleground. Flight teams of scout aircraft were called "White Teams," while gunship sections were called "Red Teams." Combining them produced "Pink Teams," which proved highly effective.

Bell OH-13Ss and Hiller OH-23Gs pioneered the scout role in Vietnam prior to the arrival of the Hughes OH-6A. This weary OH-13 was manned by a pilot and gunner operating an infantry-style M-60A machine gun suspended in the doorway. Smoke grenades are carried in a rack outside the aircraft. Immediately aft of the gunner's position is the yellow marking of B Troop, 1st Squadron, 9th Cavalry, 1st Cavalry Division. On the plexiglas nose is a Confederate flag and the name "Dixie Bell." (Melvin Edwards)

OH-13S of the 1st Cavalry Division at An Khe in the Central Highlands in January 1968. Blue and yellow bands on the forward skids emphasize the importance the Army placed upon color markings to identify units in Vietnam. (Robert Steinbrunn)

Unlike many Loaches in Vietnam, this OH-6A (s/n 68-17365) survived long enough to wear three personal names. After "Electric Olive II," number 365 was named "Enforcer," then "Dark Death." It is seen here in February 1972 with C Troop, 16th Cavalry manned by Rod Willis (right seat), Hugh Mills, and Terry Davis in the rear. The wording "Bobb the Toad" on the front door frame stood for Bob Todd, the aircraft's former pilot. (James Sheetz)

A Loach of Apache Troop, 7th Squadron. 1st Cavalry flies near the Vietnam-Cambodia border, west of Moc Hoa, during the Cambodian incursion in late 1970. (Bill Staffa)

On a landing zone near the Cambodian border in 1966, a captured suspected member of the Viet Cong awaits transportation in a 1st Cavalry OH-13S. Bell OH-13S and Hiller OH-23G helicopters pioneered the Aeroscout role in Vietnam until arrival of the OH-6A Loach. (Ed Lemp)

In June 1968, members of Headquarters Company, 1st Brigade, 1st Cavalry Division modified a rocket launcher for one of their OH-13s. Though successful, it was ordered removed. The pilot, Frank Vanatta, poses with his rocket-armed Sioux at LZ Betty. (Frank Vanatta Collection)

Besides visual recon, Loaches flew a wide variety of missions, including bomb damage assessment, landing zone recon, convoy cover, sensor operations, target acquisition and screening for ground troops. They were even pressed into service for re-supply and rescue.

Loaches flew with a crew of two or three, depending largely upon unit policy, which centered around use of the XM-27 minigun system. Going face-to-face with the enemy required massive firepower, which countered the OH-6A's original intended use as an observation platform. Some unit commanders insisted that Loaches only do observation, while others felt the scouts should slug it out with the enemy they encountered. The minigun system's weight restricted the crew to two, meaning the pilot flew right seat, with the gunner/crew chief to his left. Often, the minigun was omitted in favor of a third crewman, who served as a third, more flexible gun. Besides the gunners' stripped down M-60 machine guns, some units added firepower with experimentally mounted rocket launcher tubes.

Crew chiefs and observers were responsible for scouting and covering their fields of fire. The more proficient they were, the easier it was for the pilot, who had to simultaneously scout, fly the aircraft, talk on the radio, and fire the minigun. Pilots often taught their crewmen how to fly the Loach in the event they were wounded or killed. Most scout enlisted crewmen, who were dubbed "Torques" or "Oscars," were experienced infantrymen, had attended the Scout Observer Course, or had combat flight experience.

True to their proud scout lineage of frontier days, scout crewmen became expert at reading "sign," to the extent of knowing the signs and habits of the enemy. Details such as bent grass, footprints, and camouflaged positions seldom escaped a skilled scout. Often, the enemy stayed hidden, relying instead on booby traps in trees. Some times a downed Loach served as bait for the rescue forces the enemy knew would come. It was not unusual for veteran scout pilots to be shot down multiple times. Rod Willis and his crew chief, Ken Stormer of C/16 were shot down three times in one day, only to be rescued and flown back to base to grab another Loach.

Late in the war, some OH-6As were modified with an exhaust diffuser system to counter heat-seeking missiles. The NVA used the missiles during the battle of Kontum in 1972, during which Loaches were hit 42 times. Nine were lost during the four-month battle, eight alone from H troop, 17th Cavalry. The aeroscouts paid a heavy price for engaging in one of the most hazardous flying duties of the war. Losses were extremely high, with 842 OH-6As destroyed.

Despite the OH-6A's remarkable achievements, and the respect it had earned, it was destined for replacement. Bells' OH-58A "Kiowa" arrived in Vietnam early in 1970, and by March there were 160 in country. Aircrew who had become partial to the OH-6A found the Kiowa ill-suited for the scout role. The OH-58A was heavier and could not match the OH-6A's speed and agility. It did, however, offer more crew comfort, improved avionics, and good handling at low speeds. Although many OH-58As in Vietnam ended up in utility and transport roles, some air cavalry units found them successful as scout aircraft. A total of 45 OH-58As were lost during the war, 28 of them at the enemies' hand.

(Above) Besides the name "Captain America," this OH-6A (s/n 67-16023) features brightly painted skid gear at Duc Pho in 1970. (Robert Brackenhoff)

(Left) A member of D Troop's Aero Rifle Platoon shows off an enemy SKS rifle and pistol captured during an attack by Aeroscouts in August 1969. An Aeroscout pilot in the background carries a .45 Cal. Thompson sub-machine gun. (Hugh Mills)

Since losses of medical evacuation helicopters were high, the 101st Airborne Division's 326th Medical Battalion relied on the OH-6A's speed and agility for the dangerous job. It too, however, was shot down in 1969 after 20 missions. This Loach (s/n 67-16254) is the only dedicated medevac OH-6A known to have existed during the war. (Joe Campbell)

Aeroscout crew chief/gunners in Vietnam were known as "Oscars" or "Torques," depending on unit. These highly trained, volunteer observer/gunners, along with their pilot and the aircraft, functioned as a single unit in the low-level, high-threat environment. This C Troop, 16th Cavalry Oscar poses in 1971 with the OH-6A's minigun and a "Free 60," which was a cut-down infantry-style M-60A machine gun. (James Sheetz)

The typical Loach observer/gunner's work station comprised a "Free 60," ammunition box, smoke grenades hung on a wire, and personal weapons, such as an M-16 rifle and M-79 grenade launcher. (Joe Crockett)

Like the OH-6A, its successor, the Bell OH-58A also flew without doors in Vietnam. Despite its positive features, the OH-58 would never endear itself to the majority of aircrew and ground troops in Vietnam, as did the OH-6A. This 17th Cavalry OH-58A "Kiowa" departs Quang Tri in 1971. (Robert Brackenhoff)

Often, Army aircraft in Vietnam were stranger than many of the missions they flew. The unit and mission of this OH-6A at Tan Son Nhut AB in 1971 remains unexplained. The aircraft's unusual camouflage and absence of markings puts it in the category of countless special operations conducted by Army aviation during the war. (Rich Jalloway)

Wearing the name "Challenger" and specially-painted skid gear, this OH-6A (s/n 67-16524) stands by at Duc Pho in 1970. Windows above the rear cabin were painted over to prevent the sun and spinning rotor blades from interfering with the gunner's vision. (Robert Brackenhoff)

"Borrowed Time" was just one example of how Army aircrew beefed up the firepower of their aircraft. This Loach of D Troop, 3rd Squadron, 4th Cavalry, often called "Three-Quarter Cav," was armed with a hand-operated 7.62mm minigun. (David Atkinson)

Classified Secret

Often overlooked is Army Aviation's intelligence-gathering community, which was present throughout the war. Such oversight may be due, in part, to the Army's avoidance of advertising those special units, from which today's Army intelligence-gathering program has evolved.

Battlefield doctrine dictates that commanders strive to find out where the enemy is and what he is doing. Aircraft specially modified with intelligence-collecting equipment have proven to be the best means of gathering such information. The war in Southeast Asia became a valuable testing ground for such electronic technology, which had been cultivated since the Korean war. Although the importance of Airborne Radio Detection Finding (ARDF) was realized as far back as World War Two, it wasn't until 1961 that a system was used successfully aboard an aircraft. The Army's involvement with *electronic warfare,* which actually began during the 1950s, gained momentum with the impending commitment to the worsening situation in Vietnam.

Thus began in earnest the Army's vast program of airborne intelligence-gathering, conducted under its low-profile Army Security Agency (ASA). The ASA was one aspect of *Operation White Oak,* the code name for the effort by the National Security Agency (NSA) to gather intelligence on North Vietnam. The 400th USASA Operations Unit was activated in May 1961 using the cover designation 3rd Radio Research Unit. *Radio Research (RR)* would come to identify all ASA units throughout the conflict. The aircraft and their systems were identified by a variety of zany code names and abbreviations, which were based upon the letter groups *LEF, LAF, CEF,* and *CAF* used by the ASA.

Although overshadowed by more popular aircraft, ASA aircraft and their crews flew unarmed and suffered losses while writing the most unusual chapter in Army aviation history. The mission of Radio Research crews fell under the heading *Signal Intelligence (SIGINT),* meaning that they eavesdropped on and recorded enemy radio traffic, and pinpointed the location of enemy transmitters. This information was sent directly to the National Security Agency at Fort Meade, Maryland. The ability to obtain such vital information would mean thousands of lives saved during the course of the war. After experimenting with several types of fixed-wing aircraft, the Army found most favorable de Havilland's L-20A (U-6A) Beaver equipped with a rudimentary ARDF system. In early 1962 three systems were hand-carried to Vietnam for installation in three L-20As loaned to the 3rd Radio Research unit from the MACV-MAAG Flight Detachment.

In September the first Grumman OV-1 Mohawks arrived to conduct surveillance, although they did not operate as dedicated intelligence-gathering platforms. The Beavers later were designated RU-6As, and were joined in mid-1963 by seven RU-6As, which were code-named *Seven Roses.* Pleased with the results of the RU-6As, Army Aviation leaders embarked on an elaborate intelligence-gathering program, which, at its peak, boasted a total of 80 fixed-wing aircraft and five helicopters in theater. Aircrews flew a variety of aircraft modified with electronic systems developed in the laboratories of the ASA, the Electronics Warfare Laboratory, the U.S. Army Electronics Command, the Signal Corps, and private contractors.

The first ARDF systems comprised a C-12 compass, two standard Collins receivers, and dipole antenna mounted at each wing tip. When the 3rd Radio Research Unit's Aviation Section

An RU-8D (s/n 56-3712) about 1967. Large flat black blade antennae, called "Winebottle," replaced smaller "Broomstick" types. Beech U-8 "Seminoles" in the Army inventory found extended lives in the field of Radio Research. (Terry Love)

After 1965, Radio Research aircraft appeared in overall flat Olive Drab, with black figures. The fuselage upper sections were painted Gloss White to reflect solar heat, thereby preventing electronic equipment from overheating. This RU-8D (s/n 58-3060) of the 146th Radio Research Company wears the emblem of its parent unit, the 224th Army Security Agency Battalion, on its tail fin. (John B. Hyde)

Of 34 RU-21Ds, 18 were U-21As modified with improved cockpits, avionics and sensor equipment. Its propellers bent as the result of a belly landing at Chu Lai in February 1971, this was one of 18 RU-21Ds code-named Laffing Eagle, which evolved from the RU-8D. This RU-21D (s/n 67-18105) was named "Humpin' Motha." (Robert Brackenhoff)

"Pathfinder" was a one-of-a-kind radio direction finding system installed in Caribou s/n 62-4147. Designated an RCV-2B, the Caribou was damaged by ground fire and later was included in the Caribou transfer to the Air Force. (Stephen Miller)

RU-8Ds of the 146th RR Co. wait at Tan Son Nhut AB in 1966. Barely visible in the distance are six U-8Fs of the MACV Flight Detachment. (Terry Love)

was officially established in June 1963, the Beavers were joined by the second ARDF conversion; two Beech RU-8Ds and an RU-8F. Improvements in the U-8 Seminole series included a Doppler navigation system, which provided the crew with a constant, precise location reference, necessary when working over rough terrain, unlike the flat Delta where the Beavers operated.

A bombsight device mounted in the rear of the aircraft enabled the operator to guide the pilot over a specific point. Later, the wing-mounted dipole antennae were changed from the "broomstick" type to a flat blade type called "wine bottle." All RU-8Ds, which first appeared in 1959 under the designation RL-23D, had wing extensions. Most of the 20 original examples mounted either the APS-85 or APQ-86 Side-Looking Airborne Radar. At least one dozen RU-8Ds were equipped with radio tracking gear, called *Short Skirt*, and later *Lefair Knee*. The crews of RU-8Ds in Vietnam were made up of a pilot, copilot, mission plotter, and radio operator. The RU-6As carried a crew of three. Missions lasting between four and five hours were flown throughout entire Corps areas.

In January 1966 the 146th Radio Research Company was assigned a one-of-a-kind high frequency ARDF system installed in de Havilland Caribou serial number 62-4147. Designated an RCV-2B and code named *Pathfinder*, the Caribou flew with four operators, besides its normal crew of three. On a mission north of the DMZ, the Caribou flew into a flak trap, where it was raked by .30 cal fire. A 37mm shell tore through the Caribou's tail, jamming the rudder. The aircraft was flown to Dong Ha and then back to Phu Bai. It was repaired and in 1967 became part of the Caribou transfer to the Air Force.

Radio Research units later received additional RU-6As, plus RU-8Ds equipped with ARD-15 electronics, called *Checkmate*. These were followed by RU-8D conversions labeled *Winebottle* and *Cefish Person*. Eventually, a total of 54 RU-8Ds and 34 RU-6As were on the Army inventory, emphasizing the importance of the ARDF mission in Vietnam.

The second generation of ARDF systems centered around the Beech U-21 series of aircraft, which was larger than the U-8 and featured higher performance. An early attempt to create a fully integrated DF, intercept, and jamming system, which was called *Crazy Dog* and later *Cefirm Leader*, began in 1967. Nine aircraft, using three RU-21A, B, and C models, had the V-SCANDARF system installed. The concept was not as effective as designers had hoped, nevertheless, the RU-21Bs and Cs were sent to Vietnam. Exceptional results were obtained with the RU-21D configuration, called *Laffing Eagle*, which was a more direct descendant of the RU-8D. Besides expanding frequency coverage and the addition of a second operator, the RU-21D used an internal navigation system (INS) in place of the RU-8D's Doppler, and V-SCAN, which gave 240-degree DF coverage. The first *Laffing Eagle* aircraft arrived in Vietnam in December 1968.

Next came *Left Jab*, which was the first Army system capable of 360-degree DF coverage, and the most sophisticated system fielded by the ASA in Vietnam. Installed in JU-21A aircraft, this also was the first use of a computer to store data and pinpoint signal emissions detected by the INS and DF antennae. Three JU-21As

This was one of three JU-21A Left Jab platforms used by the ASA in Vietnam to intercept and locate enemy VHF radio transmissions. Serial number 67-18063's direction-finding antenna was housed in a retractable pod on the aircraft's belly. (Dennis Buley Collection)

The Lockheed AP-2E, BuNo. 131531 goes through a run-up check in 1969. The nose wheel door was extended to accommodate a ladder providing access to the electronics bay. Number 531 wore a purple heart ribbon after it was hit by anti-aircraft fire in April 1969. (Ed Jones)

Of the Neptunes flown by the "Crazy Cats," BuNo. 131492 remained basically a stock SP-2E, retaining the clear nose and ASW radome. The unique 1st RR Co. emblem was designed by MGM Studios and features the character "Tom" of the Tom and Jerry cartoons. (Ed Jones)

were built, all of which were assigned to the 138th RR Co. at Phu Bai in early 1971. On 4 March, one of the trio and crew, using the call sign "Vanguard 216," found what they were looking for on a mission to collect intelligence on SAM sites in the northern regions of the DMZ. A SAM was launched, finding its mark on the aircraft and its five-man crew.

A refined version of *Laffing Eagle*, called *Left Foot,* combined *Laffing Eagle's* DF gear with the *Left Jab* computer, and faced the operators forward. The aircraft, 16 of which were built, was dubbed RU-21E and was externally indistinguishable from the RU-21D.

A number of incidents underscored the danger of Radio Research missions, which were usually flown alone and unarmed. Besides the loss of Vanguard 216, fixed-wing losses include the disappearance of an RU-6A on 15 November 1966, an RU-8D crash near Da Nang on 29 December 1967, and an RU-6A collision with a VNAF Huey near Can Tho on 24 November 1970, killing all aboard. On 12 February 1969, an RU-1A was shot down over Cambodia. The crew of four was captured and turned over to the Cambodian government. They were released one month later after President Richard Nixon apologized for violating Cambodian airspace.

Helicopter ARDF assets in Vietnam were few compared to fixed-wing. Five UH-1D Hueys were modified and called *Left Bank.* Three were assigned to the 371st RR Co. in July 1967. Named "The Good," "The Bad," and "The Ugly," they were attached to the 1st Cavalry Division. The remaining two were assigned to the 374th RR Co. supporting the 4th Infantry Division. *Left Bank* Hueys saw extensive service locating and monitoring enemy units that were targeted for B-52 strikes. In 1969 the *Left Bank* system was installed in newer UH-1H aircraft, two of which were shot down, resulting in eight crew deaths. Before an improved *Left Bank II* system could be deployed, the withdrawal from Vietnam had begun, ending the project.

Most unusual among the ASA's widespread electronic warfare program was the *Ceflein Lion* project, better known as *Crazy Cat.* In 1966 a Department of Defense study, code-named *Jayson East,* set as its goal electronically isolating North Vietnam from elements in the south by intercepting and jamming radio communications.

The search began for a branch of service that wanted the task, and a large airplane that not only could hold the large equipment package, but remain on-station for extended periods. With a foothold in the field of electronic intelligence (ELINT), the Army saw the venture as worthwhile, despite the feud with the Air Force over large airplanes. Since the Caribou was the largest airplane in the Army inventory, it was the obvious choice for installation of the mission package. When the Army relinquished the Caribou to the Air Force, the ASA set its sights on the Navy's Lockheed P-2 "Neptune."

The importance of the mission overrode the Caribou transfer agreement, but to avoid another political battle, the program was not revealed to the Air Force. Army enlisted personnel sent to NAS Jacksonville found their most difficult task avoiding questions as to why they were being trained as plane captains for a large Navy aircraft. Almost all the aircrew selected for the *Crazy Cat* project were seasoned in multi-engine aircraft, and were on their second enlistment. Some came from within the ASA. Pilot training was conducted by the Navy's VP-31 at NAS North Island. Since the 1st Aviation Company was losing its Caribous, it was selected to become the 1st Radio Research Company (Aviation), assigned six

The AP-2E BuNo. 131526 was one of three "Active" Electronic Warfare platforms of the 1st RR Co. It is seen here at Iwakuni, Japan in 1968. (Yamauchi/Tom Doll)

SP-2E Neptunes.

The aircraft, which used the designations AP-2E and RP-2E interchangeably, were the largest and heaviest aircraft the Army had ever flown, its first four-engine aircraft since 1948, and its first with jet engines. After modifications at Convair's San Diego facility, three Neptunes were converted to *Active* jamming platforms, and two became *Passive* listening platforms. The sixth aircraft, called the "Bounce Bird," after having its anti-submarine warfare gear removed and Army radios installed, remained basically a stock SP-2E, which was used for training and support. By 2 July 1967, the entire unit and its special Neptunes had arrived at Cam Ranh Bay, Vietnam. Like all RR aviation units in Vietnam, the 1st RR Co. had as its parent command the 224th RR Battalion of the 509th RR Group. Based at Saigon, the 509th had operational control of all ARDF assets, including USAF EC-47s, RAAF U-17s, and VNAF RU-6As.

The Crazy Cat mission was morse and voice code intercept and jamming of enemy HF and UHF radio transmissions, with emphasis on low-powered field radio intercept. Missions were usually flown with a crew of 13 or 14, including between three and seven electronic operators, a mission controller, and an equipment repairman. Voice intercept operators were Vietnamese linguists. Since missions lasted up to 15 hours, three pilots were aboard. One mission per day was flown, rotating the work between five aircraft and three crews. More missions were flown over the northern regions of South Vietnam, and some were cross-border, including over the Ho Chi Minh Trail. Using the call sign "Cat's Paw," Crazy Cats normally worked at altitudes between 8,500 and 10,500 feet.

The jamming capability of the *Crazy Cat* package was not used to the extent it was intended, due to problems with the trial system. Besides, the NSA believed that it was more important to monitor enemy transmissions than disrupt them. Power for the impressive jamming capability was derived from a bomb bay-mounted Allison T53 turbine engine, the same used to power the Army's OH-6A helicopter.

All four engines were required for takeoff since the AP-2E, with its mission gear, full fuel load, and long-range fuel tank, weighed in at over 80,000 pounds. Having only three wheels, its weight per square inch of rubber on the ground was among the highest of any aircraft. For safe operations, Army Neptunes needed runways at least 10,500 feet in length, only six of which existed in South Vietnam. Despite their age, and persistent hydraulic problems, the Neptunes served the Army well. Nevertheless, Crazy Cat crews experienced their share of mechanical woes, and scrapes with combat.

After the first mission flown by the 1st RR Co., BuNo. 131429 slid off the wet runway at Pleiku when a prop failed to reverse. The AP-2E was repaired; however, it was later damaged at Cam Ranh Bay by an enemy infiltrator, who sabotaged flight controls. On 14 April 1969, enemy gunners scored a hit on BuNo. 131531. The 37mm shell tore through the left inboard flap section and exploded above the wing. The aircraft returned safely to Cam Ranh Bay. That same Neptune, on 21 March 1969, was landed successfully by CW4 Keith Glasgow with jet engines only after both recip engines failed. Glasgow brought the hefty Neptune down with room to spare at Tuy Hoa Air Base, earning him the Distinguished Flying Cross.

Before the war ended, advancing technology caught up with the Neptunes, which were replaced by smaller aircraft equipped with smaller systems requiring fewer operators. Before the last Crazy Cat mission was flown on 31 March 1972, the unit had amassed nearly 46,000 hours, and had surpassed a mission flight time of 17 hours without refueling.

The four Radio Research Companies flying smaller fixed-wing aircraft left Vietnam during 1972. The two surviving *Left Jab* JU-21As stayed longer, flying the last ASA mission on 16 February 1973. Both were then assigned to the 7th RR Field Station at Udorn Royal Thai Air Force Base, finally leaving Southeast Asia in April 1975.

Probably the least known and most highly classified electronic surveillance performed by Army personnel in the Pacific was called *Farm Team*. Called *Sea Brine* by the Navy, this telemetry intelligence system was a joint Army/Navy program, which had its origins in the late 1950s. To monitor the important telemetry communications that followed missile launches, Navy Fleet Air Reconnaissance Squadrons VQ-1 and VQ-2 flew Douglas A3D-2Q (later EA-3B) aircraft directly towards the signal source. Aboard the "Whales" were Army Security Agency operators assigned to Special Activities Detachments (SAD) 1 and 2.

Although the details of SAD-1's activities remain classified, it is known that the unit consisted of two nine-man teams, each with an officer, an NCO, and seven operators. Although SAD-1 was based at NAS Atsugi, Japan, missions were flown from all over the Pacific, normally rotating crews every six weeks. The main *Farm Team* aircraft was EA-3B BuNo. 146449, which normally flew missions with a Navy pilot, navigator, plane captain, and four ASA signal intercept operators. The Navy aircrew wings worn by these Army operators often raised many questions. A second EA-3B, BuNo. 142673, was acquired in 1969 when SAD-2 at Ramstein AB, in West Germany ceased operation. Other than a TA-3B, Farm Team EA-3Bs were the only "long-nosed Whales" in the squadron.

Believed to have been initially activated in 1963 or 1964, SAD-1 was inactivated in November 1974. Its electronics were shipped off to Berlin, while the aircraft itself returned to VQ-1's facility in Guam.

Besides their contribution to the development of today's sophisticated electronic intelligence systems, the most significant achievement of Army Security Agency aircrews is the thousands of lives saved as a result of their skill and dedication.

Vietnam-based Radio Research Units

UNIT	LOCATION	AIRCRAFT
1st RR Co.	Cam Ranh Bay	AP-2E/RP-2E
138th RR Co.	Da Nang, later Phu Bai	RU-8D and RU-21
144th RR Co.	Can Tho, later Nha Trang, later Da Nang	RU-6A and RU-8D
146th RR Co.	Cam Ranh Bay, later Tan Son Nhut, later Long Thanh	RU-6A, RU-1A, RU-8D, RU-21
156th RR Co.	Long Thanh North, later Can Tho	RU-8D, RU-21; OV-1

Just prior to the infusion of fixed-wing surveillance aircraft to the war effort, the Army tested a series of drones, whose course could be pre-programmed or radio-controlled. This was Republic's AN/USD-3 "Snooper," powered by a Continental piston engine, giving the 1,000-pound drone a range of 100 miles at 300 mph at a ceiling of 20,000 feet. Its nose section could house photographic, infrared, radar, or TV reconnaissance systems. The Snooper was recovered by parachute and was equipped with inflatable bags to ensure soft landings. A total of 50 SD-3s were built for the Army. (U.S. Army)

Army pilot John B. Hyde poses with an RU-6A (s/n 53-7957) of the 146th RR Co. in July 1970. The Beaver mounts several antennas and wears a Snoopy character on the engine cowling. (John B. Hyde Collection)

Mounting dipole antennas on the wings, and its fuselage upper surfaces painted white to reflect solar heat, an RU-1A of the 146th RR Co. is seen in 1970. (John B. Hyde)

Numerous antennas are visible on AP-2E BuNo. 131531 as it departs Cam Ranh Bay in 1970. (U.S. Army)

Wearing few markings, this EA-3B (BuNo. 146449) was the primary Farm Team aircraft, which carried Army Security Agency operators throughout the Pacific to monitor missile launch telemetry communications during the Vietnam war. The special aircraft, seen here in 1971, was flown by Navy Fleet Air Reconnaissance Squadron VQ-1. (Toshiyuki Toda)

Snakes

The element most difficult to incorporate into the air assault/airmobile concept was the armed helicopter. Although the Army had become adept at modifying aircraft with weapons, it took the Vietnam war to spawn the pure helicopter gunship; one designed and built solely for helicopter escort and direct fire support. With an eye on the worsening situation in Vietnam, and mindful of the Army's experiments with arming helicopters, the Bell Helicopter Company in Spring 1965 began in-house research and development of an advanced attack helicopter that made use of UH-1 Huey components. Although previous Bell attack helicopter designs stirred little interest among Army officials, they reconsidered as the war intensified. Faced with the decision either to halt their *Advanced Aerial Fire Support System* program, lower its requirements, or select an aircraft that could quickly go into production, they chose Bell's Model 209. The new design, which was re-designated AH-1G HueyCobra, featured a narrow fuselage that positioned the pilot behind and above the gunner/pilot, stub wings with ordnance hard points, and a chin turret housing a GAU-2B/A 7.62mm minigun. The Lycoming T-53 series turbine engine, carried over from the Huey line, drove a transmission and 540 rotor system already proven in the UH-1C.

In anticipation of HueyCobra deliveries, the Army's Aviation Material Command established the AH-1G New Equipment Training Team (NETT) on 1 August 1966. To fulfill the NETT's twofold mission of learning the aircraft and training future instructors, 36 combat-experienced pilots, mechanics and specialists began duty at Bell's plant in April 1967. On 28 August, the select team, along with 15 civilian specialists from Bell, Emerson Electric, and Avco's Lycoming Division, loaded 12 AH-1Gs and a UH-1D Huey aboard Air Force cargo aircraft for the flight to Bien Hoa Air Base, South Vietnam.

The HueyCobra made its first flight in Vietnam on 31 August and four days later drew first blood. Major General George P. Seneff, Jr., commander of the 1st Aviation Brigade and an early proponent of the AH-1G, and his pilot, CW2 John D. Thompson, in s/n 66-15263, diverted from their routine flight to join Huey gunships engaging the enemy near Can Tho in the Mekong Delta. When Seneff and Thompson took a Viet Cong sampan under fire during the much publicized event, they were credited with the HueyCobra's first kill. The mission was especially rewarding for General Seneff since two years earlier, as Director of Army Aviation, he faced stiff opposition within the Army's command structure to acquisition of the AH-1G.

The Cobra NETT's first students were from the 1st Platoon "Playboys" of the 334th Aerial Weapons Company (AWC), which had flown Huey gunships in Vietnam since 1962. The Bien Hoa-based Playboys began turning in their Hueys during September 1967, and the first class completed AH-1G transition on 4 October. Six of the originally deployed AH-1Gs became operational two days later. On the 8th a pair of Playboy HueyCobras flew the aircraft's first official combat mission, first destroying seven sampans, and later recorded 13 enemy kills while supporting a combat assault by the 118th AHC. Playboy AH-1Gs flew combat missions unopposed until 16 November, when Captain Kenneth Rubin's Cobra was downed by ground fire. Playboy crewmen began writing the book on AH-1G tactics, even performing the first medevac mission with a HueyCobra, a most unconventional tactic that other AH-1G pilots would repeat. The incident occurred at Bien Hoa AB when

Illustrating the extent to which the U.S. Army tested the armed helicopter concept prior to the AH-1G is this CH-34 (s/n 53-4493). Developed at Fort Benning, Georgia, the "Choctaw" carried two 20mm cannons, three .50 cal. machine guns, six .30 cal. machine guns, 40 2.75-inch rockets, and two 5-inch rockets, making it the most heavily armed helicopter of its day. (U.S. Army)

Two of the first batch of Cobras in Vietnam were painted with the Air Force camouflage scheme. This is s/n 66-15259 of the Cobra NETT at Bien Hoa in 1967. It was long believed that no other Cobras wore such camouflage until photographs surfaced showing similarly painted AH-1Gs of the 1st Squadron, 9th Cavalry, 1st Cavalry Division. (Floyd Werner Collection)

An AH-1G shows off its narrow frontal profile in 1970. The Snake carries XM-18 miniguns inboard on its stub wings, and 19-tube XM-200 rocket launchers outboard. The chin turret houses a minigun and a 40mm grenade launcher. The forward seated gunner's cockpit access was on the aircraft's left side, while the pilot's was opposite. (Robert Brackenhoff)

Serial no. 69-16442 first served D Company, 227th AHB, 1st Cavalry Division until May 1971, when it was transferred to the 238th Aerial Weapons Company. While with D/227, the Cobra wore this caricature of "Mister Olds" and the play on its serial number, based upon the then popular 442 muscle car built by Oldsmobile. Unit aircraft numbers were displayed as Roman numerals on the AH-1G's rotor pylon, which was referred to as the "Dog House." (Rich Jalloway)

"Pandora's Box," AH-1G s/n 68-15031, is readied for a mission in 1971. The D Company, 227th AHB, 1st Cavalry Division used Roman numerals for company aircraft numbers. (William P. White)

the enemy launched the Tet Offensive on 31 January 1968. While fellow Playboy crews provided covering fire, Capt. Rubin landed to rescue two wounded USAF security policemen pinned down by enemy fire. Rubin directed the pair to open the ammunition bay doors and climb onto them, and then flew them to safety. Playboy Cobras played a major role in defending the air base during the attack. After 36 hours of sustained combat, and with the assistance of NETT AH-1Gs and UH-1C gunships of the 68th AHC, the main assault on Bien Hoa had been beaten back. After its decisive role in defending Saigon, Long Binh, and Bien Hoa during Tet, even rival Air Force officials admitted the Cobra could do everything a fighter aircraft could do.

As more AH-1Gs were shipped to Vietnam, they filled the ranks mainly of air cavalry troops, assault helicopter companies, aerial weapons companies and aerial rocket artillery units. As Cobra crews learned the aircraft's capabilities, the book they were writing on AH-1G operations grew larger to keep pace with the ever-changing tactical environment. HueyCobras commonly engaged targets at altitudes between 1,400 and 2,000 feet, with higher altitudes possible in view of the accuracy of weapon systems. The AH-1G's high speed, agility and slim frontal profile made it a difficult target for enemy gunners. Relying on the "Snake's" speed of 190 knots in a dive, pilots often over-flew targets, and enemy gunners knew that to fire on the *skinny helicopter* meant certain death.

Despite the AH-1G's popularity, some crews had reservations about its combat effectiveness. Some Huey drivers-turned-Cobra-pilots had come to rely heavily on the eyes, ears, and versatility of door gunners. The AH-1G's nearly soundproof cockpit made it difficult for pilots to detect ground fire. Even after amassing combat hours in the AH-1G, some pilots remained partial to the security and cohesiveness of enlisted crew. The Huey gunship versus Cobra argument thrived throughout the war. The few drawbacks to the AH-1G centered around its cockpit. It was discovered that a blue tint applied to early models not only reduced vision at night, but increased interior glare and reflections, which dangerously disoriented pilots. And Vietnam's oppressive heat drove temperatures in the sealed cockpit unbearably high until a powerful air conditioner was installed.

Many times more lethal than its namesake, the Cobra's bite came mainly from miniguns, both in the chin turret and in XM-18 pods under the wings. The TAT-102 single-minigun turret was replaced in favor of an XM-28 turret system incorporating either two miniguns or one gun and a 40mm grenade launcher. Rocket launchers were standard 7-tube or 19-tube types. To give the AH-1G a standoff capability against .51 cal. weapons, a 20mm cannon modified for the AH-1G was introduced to the theatre during late 1969. Called the XM-35 system, the weapon required additional wiring, along with ammunition containers attached to both sides of the fuselage, and heavy panels on the fuselage to prevent muzzle blast damage. Weapon combinations and tactics varied according to

In May 1972 enemy gunners near An Loc downed this Cobra, which tried to reach the airstrip at Lai Khe. The AH-1G belonged to F Battery, 79th Artillery (ARA), which formed at Bien Hoa with F/77 to support the 1st Cavalry's 3rd Brigade. (Mike Sloniker)

The AH-1G (s/n 68-15111) at Duc Pho in 1970. On 23 March 1971, while assigned to A Troop, 1st Squadron, 9th Cavalry, it was shot down by an outgoing ARVN artillery round during a mission in Cambodia. Both pilots were killed. (Robert Brackenhoff)

unit policy, terrain and tactical requirements.

The 235th AWC flew fire teams mixed with UH-1Cs and AH-1Gs until January 1968, when it became the first all-Cobra unit in Vietnam. The following month, the 1st Cavalry Division received its first HueyCobras, which equipped the 1st Squadron, 9th Cavalry (1/9), and D Company, 229th Assault Helicopter Battalion (D/229). While other Cobra units operated with fire teams of two Snakes, or three to form a heavy fire team, 1/9 introduced the use of AH-1Gs for reconnaissance. Teaming a Cobra from its *red* gun platoon with a Hughes OH-6A Loach from its *white* aeroscout platoon resulted in a *pink* team. This tightly knit pair became an effective "Hunter-Killer" team. The idea behind *aerial rocket artillery* was to have AH-1Gs provide heavy firepower beyond the range of ground artillery batteries.

Nearly 40 units would fly the Cobra throughout Vietnam, although not all would fully replace Huey gunships. The eight assault helicopter companies that operated Cobras typically had four or six assigned, while all other units carried between eight and twelve on their inventories. Units due to receive AH-1Gs sent their pilots and ground crews to the Cobra Transition School at Vung Tau. The school's AH-1Gs formed the 5th Aviation Detachment of the 1st Aviation Brigade. The first assault helicopter companies to receive AH-1Gs were the 114th and 187th, whose deliveries began in February 1969. Bell representatives attached to the 114th were so impressed with the success of the unit's UH-1B gun platoon, named the "Cobras," that they christened the AH-1G "Cobra." Cobras were not limited to escort and hunter-killer missions. The 361st AWC, for example, first used its AH-1Gs for convoy escort, and in May 1969 began flying support for MACV-SOG teams operating in Laos and Cambodia from Forward Operating Base II, Kontum. The 361st "Pink Panthers" became the only Cobra unit dedicated to providing continuous SOG support, committing two light fire teams to SOG's Command and Control Central (CCC). The three Cobra-equipped batteries of 4th Battalion, 77th Field Artillery (ARA) of the 101st Airborne Division provided rotational support for SOG's CCN during 1969 and 1970.

The 1st Cavalry Regiment traces its lineage back to the early 19th Century Indian wars, when it was called "Dragoons." That lineage was respectfully recognized in the use of Native American troop names and emblems. This Cobra belonged to A Troop, 7th Squadron, 1st Cavalry Regiment "Blackhawks." (Cespedes/Davis)

Cobras' missions ranged from small unit action to major offensives, such as the Cambodian Incursion in May 1970. The North Vietnamese Spring Offensive in 1972 set the stage for the first Cobra-versus armor confrontation, with the Cobra coming out on top. Credit for proving the Snake's tank-busting capability goes to D Troop, 1st Squadron, 1st Cavalry; F Troop, 4th Cavalry; F Troop, 9th Cavalry, and especially F Battery, 79th Field Artillery, 1st Cavalry's 3rd Brigade, whose crews destroyed or incapacitated, mainly with rockets, more than 20 armored vehicles. The battle at An Loc pitched Cobras against intense anti-aircraft fire, which included heat-seeking SA-7 surface-to-air (SAM) missiles, necessitating hurried modification of the AH-1G's exhaust system. Most effective was an upturned exhaust pipe that directed exhaust heat into the main rotor, thereby reducing infrared signature. The installation's compromise, a common occurrence with aircraft modifications, was a slight reduction in performance and ordnance weight. To counter SAM guidance systems, an ALQ-44 unit was added to both Cobras and Hueys late in the war. The only other major modification during the war had the Cobra's tail rotor repositioned to the right side to improve directional control.

At the war's peak, nearly 700 AH-1Gs were in Vietnam. During the seven years that Cobras flew combat missions, a total of 279 were lost to both operational causes and hostile fire.

Rocket- and minigun-armed Snakes of C Troop, 7th squadron, 1st Cavalry “Comanche” head for trouble during late 1968. (Bell Helicopter)

The 20mm XM-35 system was introduced in Vietnam in late 1969 to counter the increasing presence of .51 cal. heavy machineguns. The modified M-61 Vulcan cannon fired 750 rounds-per-minute, fed by two containers on each fuselage side. A seven-tube XM-157 rocket launcher usually occupied the outboard station. This AH-1G of C Troop, 16th Cavalry is seen at Quang Tri in early 1971. (Robert Brackenhoff)

An early model AH-1G of the 7th Armored Squadron, 1st Cavalry. Early-model Cobras are differentiated from later models by their nose landing lights and left-side tail rotors. The elevator and tail fin tips of this rocket- and minigun-armed Cobra are painted white. (Larry Davis Collection)

(Above) Each Cobra unit in Vietnam that used the popular shark mouth was distinguished by different styles of the ferocious marking. This shark mouth version identified D Troop, 1st Squadron, 10th Cavalry. (William P. White)

(Right) Personnel of A Troop, 7th Squadron, 1st Cavalry with one of their Cobras. "Apache" Troop AH-1Gs wore their company emblem on the aircraft's "dog house." (Floyd Werner Collection)